# Devon
# MURDERS

John Van der Kiste

SUTTON PUBLISHING

First published in the United Kingdom in 2006 by
Sutton Publishing Limited · Phoenix Mill
Thrupp · Stroud · Gloucestershire · GL5 2BU

British Library Cataloguing in Publication Data
A catalogue record for this book is available from the British Library.

ISBN 0-7509-4408-0

All illustrations are from the author's collection unless otherwise credited.

Typeset in 10.5/13.5pt Sabon.
Typesetting and origination by
Sutton Publishing Limited.
Printed and bound in England by
J.H. Haynes & Co. Ltd, Sparkford.

# CONTENTS

# FOREWORD

Life in country areas, it has been said, tends to generate less of the pressure that leads to violence. Because of this, it should follow that the largely rural county of Devon has seen fewer murder cases than more urbanised parts of England. But both town and country areas in this corner of the British Isles have seen and reported their fair share of fatal husband-and-wife disputes, robbery with violence, baby farming and episodes of insanity with dire consequences. In September 1866, shortly after the murder of William Ashford and the Torquay baby-farming scandal had kept both local and national press and their readers agog, *The Times* was moved to record that 'Devon, the fairest county in England, outwardly seems to be rapidly attaining a reputation among the worst.' Less than twenty years later the same 'fairest county' witnessed one of the most celebrated true crime stories of all, in which the man found guilty and sentenced to death went down in history as 'the man they could not hang'.

I hope the pages that follow will provide a satisfactory, and dare I say it entertaining, account of some of the cases that have regrettably tarnished Devon's reputation over the years.

Any writer embarking on such a book cannot but acknowledge the work of previously published authors who have paved the way. I would like to record my thanks to Judy Chard, John J. Eddleston, Steve Fielding, Grant John Harrison, Paul Harrison and Colin Wilson, all of whom have been responsible for earlier titles on Devon murders, or exhaustive works of reference covering murder on a national basis. Their books, and others used, are recorded in the bibliography.

Among those who have been kind enough to help with personal advice and providing material are Sue Fletcher, Nicola Sly, Shirley Stapley, Graham Brooks, PC Simon Dell, Stewart Evans, Chris Graves, Steve Johnson, Dr Ian Mortimer, Paul Rendell, Tony Southern, Ken Wakeling, Greg Wall, the staff at Plymouth and Exeter Local Studies libraries, and at Ford Park Cemetery Trust, Plymouth. There are others who have specifically asked not to be named but to whom I am eternally grateful nonetheless. My wife Kim not only valiantly put up with a husband whose bedside reading for several weeks revolved around titles such as *Encyclopaedia of Executions*, but also helped generously with interest, suggestions, photographing relevant scenes (in all weathers) and research both online and offline. She and my mother Kate both provided invaluable advice, encouragement and research, and their reading through of the manuscript in draft form materially contributed to a very

*Dartmoor Prison, Princetown. Built in 1805–6, Dartmoor's most notorious building became a criminal prison in 1850 and has remained so ever since.* (Courtesy of Ted Gosling)

much better book than might otherwise have been. Lucy Simister also read through the draft and made some very helpful comments while Hannah Lindsey Clark and James Cosgrave assisted with some of the photography.

Finally, I would like to place on record my particular thanks to my editors at Sutton Publishing, Simon Fletcher, Annabel Fearnley, Michelle Tilling, Matilda Pearce, Anne Bennett and Sarah Bryce.

# 1
# MURDER IN CHURCH

*South Brent, 1436*

The majority of facts surrounding any violent death in the fifteenth century are bound not to survive, but that does not detract from the gravity of one of Devon's most notorious murder cases, one which a contemporary, Bishop Lacey of Exeter, called 'a crime without parallel in our time and in these parts'. One evening in June 1436 the Revd John Hay, who had been Vicar of St Petroc's Church, South Brent, for eight years, was officiating at a service and had just said Vespers at the Festival of Corpus Christi, when there was a commotion in the building. One of his parishioners, Thomas Wake, entered the building, seized Hay and dragged him from the altar through a small doorway in the side of the church. There, with the help of a few partners in crime, he put the unfortunate man to death, either by beating him or stabbing him with a sword.

The nature of Wake's motive is anybody's guess. Rumour has it that though Hay was a man of the cloth, he may have been something of a womaniser, and was suspected of having an affair with Wake's wife. The latter was apprehended, and duly hanged, drawn and quartered for his sacrilegious misdemeanour. Whether any of his accomplices suffered the same fate is not recorded.

It has been claimed that South Brent shares the sorry distinction with Canterbury Cathedral of being one of only two places of worship where such a barbaric deed has occurred, the instance at Canterbury being the notorious murder of Archbishop Thomas Becket in December 1170. However, bearing in mind the savagery of the age, and the fact that it was not uncommon for those on the run and seeking sanctuary in churches to be hauled out and summarily despatched by their pursuers, it would not be surprising if a similar murder had taken place elsewhere.

On 11 September 1436, Bishop Lacey reconsecrated the church and churchyard. He also sought to draw a line under the murder by dedicating three altars.

The door through which the murderers dragged Hay is thought to have been a small opening in the north wall of the chancel, an outline of which can be seen on the outside of the building. It was bricked up when new chapels were added at a later date. Sadly, John Hay was not allowed to rest in peace. Fragments of his tomb, with recumbent effigy, were discovered in the church in 1870 – a mutilated head is now all that remains of the figure.

*The doorway of St Petroc's Church, South Brent, through which the Revd John Hay was dragged to his death. The doorway was later walled up.* (© Kim Van der Kiste)

# 2
# SET UP TO PAY THE PRICE

*Hatherleigh, 1811*

Masters often used to ask their servants to undertake rather unusual jobs, but for sheer unpleasantness few can match the despicable behaviour of Arthur Tucker, a farmer at Hatherleigh in the early years of the nineteenth century. One of his maids was Jane Cox, a spinster of about thirty who lived with her mother Mary.

Aged forty-seven, Tucker already had a wife and eight children. A couple of years earlier he had had a brief affair with Elizabeth Treneman, whom he had employed as a servant for two years. She became pregnant and gave birth to a son, John, who took his mother's surname. As soon as he knew she was expecting his child, Tucker turned Elizabeth out of the house. Mother and son lived in the nearby village of Northlew, and Tucker paid the parish authorities 1s 10d per week for their maintenance. Though he was reasonably well off, he wanted to be free of both this financial burden and the social stigma of having an unwanted child whom everybody in the area knew was his.

One day in June 1811 he came to Cox and asked her to do something for him. Ever ready to help, she accompanied him to a cowshed where he showed her a piece of paper concealing some powder in the wall. Handing it to her, he offered to pay her £1 if she would take it to young John Treneman. Cox suspected something was not quite right and, being a devout Christian, went home in tears to read her Bible. Her mother was very concerned and, being ignorant of what was going on, thought she must be ill.

Hoping Tucker would forget the errand, Cox thought no more about it for a few days. Then on 25 June she met him again and, when asked if she had done what he requested, told him she had lost the powder. He put his hand in his pocket and pulled out some more, suggesting that she should mix it with some sweets and then give it to the boy. Realising it would be difficult to get out of the deed if she wished to keep her job, she walked the 3 miles to Elizabeth Treneman's house and offered to take John out, telling his mother she wanted to buy him a present at the fair. With grave misgivings she took the little boy with her, gave him the powder and sweets, and returned him home. The powder was arsenic, and later that day he developed lockjaw.

*Exeter gaol, the scene of every execution in Devon during the nineteenth and twentieth centuries, c. 1830.*

Within a couple of hours he was dead. He was laid to rest in Hatherleigh churchyard three days later.

Cox and Tucker were both arrested and charged, the former with murder and the latter with inviting, procuring, aiding, counselling, hiring and commanding her to commit murder. At the Exeter Assizes on 9 August Cox made a full confession of her crime, which, if it had been considered carefully, amounted to little more than obeying orders from her employer, foolish and wicked though they may have been. There was no other material evidence against Tucker, and as a man of some social standing he was able to call several witnesses who testified to his good character. As a result he was acquitted.

After her arrest, Cox had confessed to committing murder, and said she did not mind being transported to any part of the world. If she had been led to believe that as an unwilling dupe she was unlikely to pay the full penalty of the law for her crime, she was to be sorely disappointed. Guilty was the verdict, and she was sentenced to be hanged at Exeter gaol on 12 August.

She was led on to the gallows, and there she addressed the crowd who had come to see her execution. She told them that Tucker had been able to persuade her to commit an abominable crime, for which she admitted she deserved to die. Her only regret was that the person who had instigated her to the commission of it was not there to share her fate with her. One can but hope that his conscience – if he had one – never ceased to trouble him afterwards. Her body was sent to a local surgeon, Robert Patch, for dissection.

# 3

# THE VIOLENT SAILOR

*Babbacombe, 1816*

In view of the exciting and often dangerous career Robert Finson led while serving in the Royal Navy during the Napoleonic Wars, it seems ironic that his ultimate fate should have been so ignominious.

Born in about 1776, he served against the Spanish in the Mediterranean Fleet in 1797 while Admiral Jervis, later Earl St Vincent, was Commander-in-Chief. Later he was involved in the blockade of Cadiz, and it was at this time that he came to meet his future brother-in-law. Both men were on board a vessel anchored off the coast of South Devon when Finson was introduced to his colleague's sister Mary and their father – they had come to visit him while he was aboard. Finson became friendly with them, and was invited to the man's wedding. Soon after this he proposed to Mary. Some of his shipmates were aware of her flighty reputation and warned him to think twice, especially as she was already carrying a child of which he was almost certainly not the father. Despite this, they were married in 1801.

During a period of peace the following year Finson was paid off by the Royal Navy. He and Mary made their home at her father's house in Babbacombe, Torquay. A young doctor made frequent visits to the family home in order to treat her father's leg, but Finson became suspicious and wondered whether the doctor was having an affair with his wife at the same time.

He became restless, and was unable to obtain the work he wanted as a mechanic. After being encouraged by his wife, who may have had her reasons for wanting her husband a good distance away, he decided to return to sea. This time he became a fisherman off the Newfoundland coast, where there was intense rivalry between the English and Portuguese. He was involved in several fights during this period, but on one occasion nearly suffered a much worse fate. During a fierce gale he was thrown overboard and driven away from the ship, but the crew saw him in time and sheared back in his direction. He was able to grab the forechains and haul himself back on the deck. There were further adventures to come, including being captured by the French and held prisoner for eighteen months.

After a while he decided that he had had enough of the seafaring life and returned home. Now he found it even harder to settle down. His mother-in-law died at about this time, and his father-in-law found endless fault with him, complaining that he was enjoying the life of a gentleman simply by living off his wife's earnings. After all Finson had been through during the previous few years, perhaps he felt he was entitled to an easier life. He thought Mary was being a spendthrift, and was annoyed that she would never tell him how she fared with the housekeeping. By this time there were two small sons to provide for as well.

The domestic arguments became more frequent and more violent. On 4 November 1816 Finson became so angered by Mary's perpetual nagging that he threw a saucepan of boiling water over her. She chased him out of the house, wielding a hatchet, shouting obscenities and threatening to cut his head off. Next day they had a quarrel about his clothes. He refused to take his shirt off for her to wash, saying there was no need as he had two in the wash already, and he did not see why he should put another clean one on until the day he was going to die. She retorted that she wished 'that would be today'.

Things quickly went from bad to worse. On the day after their public confrontation, there was a violent altercation about their ten-year-old son Robert's dog, which Finson would not allow into the house. When it came in, he chased it out, then seized young Robert and hit him about the head repeatedly for bringing the animal indoors in defiance of his orders. Next, he picked up a towel in the kitchen, wiped his hands and face, and threw it on a pile of ashes in the fireplace. When Mary asked him what he had done that for, he snapped back, 'Because I had a mind to.'

She moved closer as if to hit him, and he grabbed hold of her by the hair. In self-defence she picked up a knife and threw it at him, hitting him in the face. He checked his reflection in the mirror to see if he had been cut and finding he had not, turned to leave the house. As he did so, Mary threw a brush at him which narrowly missed him, crashing against a dresser. He threatened to knock her down, but after advancing towards her he changed his mind and turned towards the door again. She followed him outside to the gate, wielding a fender in her hand, shouting and screaming all the time. He aimed a punch at her but missed, and they went back into the house. She called him 'a murdering rogue', which ironically turned out to be the final self-fulfilling provocation. He lashed out at her, knocking her to the kitchen floor.

Young Robert and his nine-year-old cousin, Agnes Lane, watched in horror as Finson took a knife from his pocket and stabbed his wife repeatedly in the neck, chest and arm. The boy had been sitting by the fire trying to revive it with a pair of bellows; he now threw them at his father in desperation and ran off to seek help from the neighbours. Mary collapsed in the doorway and died instantly from loss of blood.

Finson wiped his bloodstained hands on Agnes's head, then ran upstairs to attack his father-in-law who was still lying in bed. After striking him with the knife and mistakenly leaving him for dead, he went downstairs again, tried to kill himself by forcing one knife after another into his chest, then crawled away to his bed to die. He came close to making a success of his suicide attempt, to the extent that his bowels were partly hanging outside his body, but he passed out and lay there unconscious until the neighbours called a doctor who came and dressed his wounds.

Two days later Mary was buried at St Mary's Church. Her husband was kept handcuffed to his bed for ten days to prevent him from doing further mischief to himself or to anyone else. He went on trial at Exeter Assizes in March 1817. One of the witnesses called was his doctor, Mr Pollard, who told the court that Finson had said his life was a burden to him and he wanted to shoot himself. Another, Mr Bailey of Devon County Hospital, said that the prisoner had been a patient there a year previously and was treated for a complaint which was probably venereal in origin. He had been unhappy, but they did not think he was insane.

The jury only took a few minutes to reach a verdict of guilty. In summing up, Mr Justice Holroyd refused to be swayed by evidence that Finson was in an abnormally low state of mind at the time of the murder, and said his actions could only be explained by 'his having given way to an unruly and brutish passion'. He was hanged on 24 March.

# 4

# THE FATAL TRIANGLE

## *Plymouth, 1818*

The relationship between Rebecca Smith, her husband Edward (a rigger), and her lover, John Green (a porter) was a peculiar one which could only ever end in tears – or worse. It was known to some of their friends and neighbours in the Dock area of Plymouth, later Devonport, that all three sometimes shared a bed. Also common knowledge was the fact that Edward would sometimes let his wife sleep with Green for the price of some beer. At one stage she left her husband and their two children and settled with Green in Ireland for about eighteen months, before returning to her husband in Plymouth.

Green evidently hoped to persuade Rebecca to return to him, and took to making a nuisance of himself by hanging around outside the Smiths' house in Fore Street. On 16 October 1817 she agreed to go with Green to his local public house, the Lion and Anchor, in Cherry Gardens Street, Plymouth

*Plymouth Dock, c. 1820.*

Dock. It was thought that she might have planned to tell him that it was all over between them.

According to Sarah Coates, the landlady, both were regular drinkers who often retired to the back parlour. On this occasion they sat drinking for about three-quarters of an hour, before Green came into the taproom to light his pipe from the fire. He then went back to join Rebecca, taking some warm beer which he said would be good for her sore mouth.

Five minutes later Rebecca staggered into the taproom, blood streaming from a severe wound in her neck. The other customers helped her into a chair and sent for a surgeon, J.G. Sparkes, to come and attend to her. By the time he arrived she was already dead. In the meantime Sarah Coates's husband Joseph, the landlord, had entered the back parlour, to find Green wiping blood from his face, hands and clothes. When Coates asked him in horror what he had done, Green replied that Rebecca Smith had tried to cut his throat, so he attacked her in self-defence.

A constable was sent for, and he decided to make a thorough search of the premises. Looking around the back parlour he found a white-handled knife, about 8 inches long, concealed beneath some paper in the grate. The point was broken off and it was still wet with blood.

Green was held in custody and tried at the Spring Assizes in March 1818. It was established that the knife belonged to Eliza Simeon, who was one of Green's fellow-lodgers, and that she had left it in his room not long before the murder took place. Anne Wilson, a neighbour of the Smiths, recalled hearing a conversation in which Rebecca had told Green that 'you mean nothing but to murder me'. Green replied, 'I value not my own life, but I don't wish to hurt you.' She reminded him that the last time he saw her, 'you said the next should be my last'.

Green's bloodstained clothes and the knife were shown to the jury. It was apparent that he had invited Rebecca to the Lion and Anchor with the intention of murdering her unless she agreed to return to him. He offered no defence or explanation in mitigation of his crime, and the jury took only a few minutes to find him guilty. Aged forty-two, he was executed at Exeter gaol on 23 March 1818.

# 5

# THE KILLING OF A MOTHER-TO-BE

*East Worlington, 1823*

In the summer of 1823 twenty-year-old farm labourer John Radford from East Worlington was told by his girlfriend, Sarah Down, that he was going to become a father in a few months' time. Radford was illegitimate himself and had never had much money to spare. From the age of seven he had been apprenticed to a local farmer, Robert Westacott, who was one of the parish overseers of the poor. That he was going to be responsible for another mouth to feed was the last news Radford wanted to hear. However, he and Sarah decided they would get married. As she had only been expecting for about six weeks, they had plenty of time.

On the evening of Friday 11 July 1823, Radford and his friend Samuel Melhuish were enjoying a drink of cider at the house of Mrs Cole at Moor End. Sarah and her sister Mary joined them later that evening and had a drink with the men. Mary went home on her own, and the others left together about a quarter of an hour later. Melhuish said goodnight to them outside the house, and left them in apparently cheerful mood.

Sarah failed to return home either that night or on Saturday. By the evening her family were becoming increasingly worried about her. As she had last been seen in Radford's company, her younger brother, John, and brother-in-law, Richard Hodge, went to his house at about 1 a.m. on Sunday. The front door was answered by Radford, who was trembling and noticeably ill at ease. He had difficulty in speaking properly, but claimed he had left Sarah at Gatton Gate on Friday night, and that was the last he saw of her. Hodge told him that he was under suspicion, and he had the choice of being taken straight to the constable at Witheridge, or coming to help them search for Sarah.

Hodge did not know the area very well, so he asked Radford to show the way. They went to the Town Moor Brakes and a lake by the river. As they walked, Hodge and Down asked Radford if he knew that Sarah was expecting his child. At first he said he did not, but when they persisted, he admitted that on the Friday night she had asked him if he was aware of the rumours about her pregnancy, which he dismissed as nonsense.

As they reached the river, Radford was recognised by William Edworthy, who said that he had just found Sarah's body. At this Radford became speechless, then burst into tears. He watched as the body was recovered from the water, denying through his tears that they had ever argued. He then admitted that he was responsible for her death, and that he had never thought of taking her life until the minute he did it. As her body was laid on the ground, he said that she had put her apron string around her neck herself in order to keep the rain off her shoulders, lest anyone should accuse him of trying to strangle her. There was a cut on her face, but he denied having struck her. A post-mortem was conducted by Mr Thomas Cross, a surgeon from Thorverton, who said that she had died from drowning and was six to eight weeks with child.

The case was disposed of relatively quickly. Radford was remanded in custody that day, Sunday 13 July. Constable Henry Burgess asked Radford if he had hurt the girl, and Radford admitted that they had been together on the Friday night. When Burgess told Radford he was sure he was 'guilty of what you are here for', Radford threw up his hands, denying that he had ever thought of committing the crime until the moment it happened: 'I was very drunk, or I should never have done it.' They had sheltered from the rain in the linhay (an open-sided agricultural building) for half an hour, he said, and then he told Sarah she ought to go home, but she was afraid to, as she and her sister would be sure to have an argument about her staying out too late. She wanted to wait a little longer until her sister was likely to be asleep. To kill time, they walked together along the riverbank. When asked whether he had thrown her in the river, and if so, whether she put up a struggle or not, Radford did not answer, merely repeating that he was drunk at the time.

The case came to trial at Exeter Assizes on 16 July. Radford was charged with having assaulted Sarah Down and deliberately causing her death by drowning. His counsel, Mr Fisher, objected that not enough time had been allowed for him to prepare for the trial. He also thought that the indictment was flawed in two aspects, namely that it was apparent that Sarah had not died merely by drowning, but that the blow to her head had contributed to her death; and that it was not stated exactly where she had died. The judge, Mr Justice Best, left the court to confer with his colleague, Mr Justice Burrough, returning to inform Mr Fisher that both objections were without foundation.

The main witnesses were Constable Burgess, who repeated everything Radford had told him since being taken into custody, and Melhuish, who confirmed that he and Radford had both drunk a quart of cider at Mrs Cole's house.

It took the jury only two minutes to deliver a verdict of guilty. In his final summing up, Burrough told Radford:

If any case of murder can be capable of aggravation, yours is that case; for it appears, from what passed early in the evening, that you led her to suppose you would make her your wife – one cannot doubt you were the father of her child; and thus, by one wicked act, you deprived one human being of existence whom you ought to have protected, and prevented another from coming into life with a similar claim upon you.

He was sent to the gallows on 28 July. As he walked out to the staircase, he told the crowds that he was 'very happy', and then said the Lord's Prayer before the noose was placed round his neck.

# 6

# FRIEND BY NAME BUT NOT BY NATURE

On 19 March 1827 Sarah Glass, a farmer at Weeks-on-the-Moor, Beaworthy, 4 miles from Okehampton, left her home on horseback to go and visit her two sons. As usual her 24-year-old daughter, also called Sarah, and her fourteen-year-old grandson, Edward (the son of one of her other children), saw her off, promising they would meet her as she returned that evening. Having spent much of the day with one son at South Yeo, she set off home at about 6.30, calling in at her other son's house in Northlew about an hour later. He rode back with her as far as Wadland Down, near her farm. It was dark by this time, and as they rode across the Down her horse suddenly reared up for no apparent reason. Sarah could not see or hear anything unusual, so she thought nothing of it as she continued on her way.

As she had expected her daughter and grandson to welcome her back, she was rather anxious when they failed to do so. Her servant and next-door neighbour, Grace Pincombe, whose husband Abraham was a labourer in Beaworthy and who also helped out on a regular basis, confirmed that they had gone to meet her. Abraham offered to go and look for them in case they had got lost, though this was unlikely since they knew the area so well. Taking a lantern with him, he wandered around, calling their names repeatedly. Getting no answer, he assumed that they must have decided to see the elder Sarah's brother at Northlew. However, it was unlike her daughter and grandson to make plans without letting her know first, and Sarah spent a sleepless night wondering where they were.

Also absent from the house, they noticed, was another servant, Thomas Friend. Aged thirty-nine, he had been in Sarah Glass's employment for about eleven years, his main job being to slaughter her pigs and sheep. As a rule he was in or near the house unless he had been sent on some particular errand. For some time he had apparently been infatuated with the younger Sarah, but she rejected his advances.

Dawn had barely broken on the Tuesday before Sarah Glass's worst fears were confirmed. The bodies of her daughter and grandson were found on Wadland Down, their throats cut, and suspicion immediately fell on the missing Friend.

*Thomas Friend.*

An inquest was held at Exeter later that morning by the coroner, Francis Kingdon. The first witness to be called, Emmanuel Tucker of Ashbury, said that he had gone out to check his wheatfields at 7 a.m. when he was alerted by his servant, Joseph Rook, who told him he had just found two bodies. He went to look, and recognised them as Sarah and Edward. Clutched in the latter's hand was a handkerchief, cut in two, which they assumed the assailant had used to stuff inside the boy's mouth in order to prevent him from screaming. Scattered beside them were various possessions including a knife, lantern, hat, bonnet, cap and comb.

Next to give evidence was Grace Pincombe. At about 2 p.m. on the previous day she had gone to North Coombe, in Bratton Clovelly, and returned about four hours later. At around 7 p.m. Friend came into the house, changed his clothes, had his supper and then went out without saying where he was going. Sarah and Edward Glass and Abraham had supper shortly afterwards, and Sarah and Edward left at about 7.30 with a lantern to meet

Mrs Glass. When Mrs Pincombe was shown the knife she said that it looked exactly like the one Friend used when he was killing pigs on the farm. Sometimes he kept it on the clock case and other times under his box in his bedroom. She had just searched for it in both places without success.

Sarah Glass then told the assembly where she had been that day, describing how her horse had taken fright on the journey back. As she went into her house at 10 p.m. she asked after her daughter and grandson, because she was so used to their coming to meet her whenever she was out visiting friends. She confirmed that Friend was not there, which was unusual. In the past she had often hemmed handkerchiefs for him, and when Tucker produced the one he had found she identified it as being one of hers. Grace Pincombe said that she had washed it several times, and knew it was one made by Mrs Glass, as it was hemmed by somebody who was left-handed. As for the weapon, Mrs Glass said it matched exactly one she had bought for Friend as a butchering knife.

Abraham Pincombe had witnessed an incident the day before between Friend and Edward Glass. The servant had lost his temper, thrown dung in the boy's face, and rubbed it in with his hands. He had then told the younger Sarah that there would never be 'any content' between them 'unless she would give her company to him', to which she told him firmly that she never would.

Dr John Fisher, a surgeon from Hatherleigh, said that he had examined both the bodies. The wound on Sarah's neck was 3 inches long and 2 inches deep, extending across the throat to the right ear, dividing the carotid artery and jugular vein. The trachea was wholly divided, as was one half of the oesophagus, exposing the cervical vertebrae. Half an inch lower down on the neck was a transverse incision through the skin, 1½ inches in length. Her hands were badly cut, probably as a result of her trying to fight off her attacker. Edward had similar wounds, but less severe. There was a bruise on the back of his head, which looked like the result of a fall, and the knees of his trousers were very dirty.

A verdict of wilful murder was returned against Friend, and the coroner issued a warrant for his arrest. He was described as 5 feet 9 inches in height, with dark hair and whiskers, and black eyes. When last seen he was wearing an unwashed, white fustian jacket, a dark striped waistcoat made of swan's down, breeches partly covered with corduroy, long gaiters, nailed shoes and a common shag hat. He had a deep cut on his left hand caused by an accident with a reap-hook, and a bruise on the forefinger of his right hand. It was assumed that he went in the direction of Plymouth, and that he would be unable to elude justice for long.

In fact, after the murders he had hidden himself in a gorse bush only about 20 yards from the farmhouse. He stayed there for a couple of days, then concealed himself in a hayloft, and after that went to a linhay in the middle of a field about 7 yards from the house. Early on the morning of 23 March William Weeks, one of the cowhands, went to do the milking and found

Friend, who said he had always intended to give himself up. He had never made any effort to escape – he had had time to put a reasonable distance between himself and the scene of the crime.

He had saved a large sum of money, perhaps in the hope of impressing Sarah Glass and assuring her that they had enough to live on should he be able to persuade her to marry him after all. It was established that he had savings amounting to £57 in the Devon & Exeter Savings Bank, and £50 was held by Mrs Glass's son Thomas, who lived at Northlew. These sums would surely have been enough had he wished to travel further afield from the West Country in the hope of escaping justice.

When he was asked what he had done, he said that after lying in wait for the younger Sarah Glass on the Down, he seized her by the clothes and killed her. Edward tried to deflect him by attacking him with a stick, but after Friend cut her throat he promptly despatched the boy as well. He expressed some contrition, especially for murdering the boy, but admitted that he had first decided upon killing Sarah earlier that evening.

An inspection of his clothes revealed bloodstains near the pocket of his jacket, and traces of blood on his breeches. He was taken to Mr J.M. Woollcombe, the local magistrate, and made a full confession, which was taken down in writing by the clerk, Charles Seymour. As Friend was illiterate, he placed his mark at the end after it had been read back to him for his approval. His version of events read thus:

That on Monday night last, the 19th inst., I left my mistress's house, called Weeks in the Moor, in Beaworthy parish, and went away across the corner of Venn Down, in the way in which people of the house generally pass. I then came up to Wadland-down, up to the gate against the inner moor, close to the corner of the wheat-field, in the parish of Ashbury. I knew they (Miss Glass and the boy) were coming that way, if they went, they were going against their mother. The mother went away to North Yeo to her son's, before us went to dinner. When I was up at the gate by the wheatfield, when I saw a candle and stopped till they came forward; when they came forward where I was, I took Miss Glass by the clothes. Then she began to throw to me and the boy. She screeched out. She said I should not kill her. I made no answer. Then I got the knife and cut Miss Glass's throat; then I went to the boy Edward and cut his throat with the same knife. I had no other. I drew the body of Miss Glass some way further down from the place where she fell. I then took up the bonnet and cloak and carried it a little further down by the hedge. I then came homewards. I went a little above-side the house into a furze-brake. I stayed there in the brake two days and two nights. Then I came out, and went away into the hay-trellet, belonging to the farm of Weeks on the Moor. I stayed there one night and one day. I went from the trellet in the evening, and went away up in a linhay adjoining a field, and there I stayed last night – there I stayed till morning, when they came to meet the cattle. Wm. Weeks came up to me at the cattle; I asked him if Mr Glass and (they) his brother Thomas was in [*sic*], for I wanted to speak with them. Then Abraham Pincombe came. Then William Weeks went in to tell Mr Glass of it. Then he came up when I was there; we came off for Ashbury. I have had nothing to eat since Monday night, until this morning. I seem I could not be easy, but that I must come in for the purpose of being taken, as I thought 'twas as well to come in first as last. I have had no promise of favour, so as to induce me to make this confession, as I was sure to be taken, and did not expect any other thing.

Obtaining a conviction was a mere legal formality, so no time was required to prepare a case for the prosecution, and the trial could therefore proceed only ten days later. Friend appeared at Exeter Spring Assizes on 27 March in front of Mr Justice Burrough. Though he had been charged with both murders, he went on trial only for the first.

In court, Abraham Pincombe testified to having seen Friend when he came in from work on the Monday afternoon and washed his hands before going out. It was the last time he saw the prisoner until Friday morning, when Weeks found him. He was in a very dazed state and would not look up at him. 'Tom, what have you done?' were Abraham's first words. 'I know my doom', was the reply. At this point in court, Friend sank down and fainted. A chair was immediately fetched for him and smelling salts were applied to his nostrils.

Next to be examined was Edward Glass, the murdered Sarah's brother. He said that Edward Weeks, William's brother, had called him out of bed and he went to the linhay, where William and Abraham were keeping an eye on Friend, who was in no state to put up any resistance. At first he was very frightened and too overcome with shock, but as soon as he could speak, he told Friend that he had ruined both their families, particularly his aged mother's. Friend said nothing until Edward Glass asked where he had been since leaving the house. He said he had spent two nights in a furze-brake and had then moved into a hayloft on the farm. On the Thursday evening he went into a wheatfield, lay down there for a while, and then moved into the linhay, where he was found. Edward wanted to know the extent of the sufferings of his sister and nephew. He also asked which of them had been the first to die.

Friend said it was Sarah whom he had killed first and he described his attack on her, telling how he had hidden behind a fence in the field as she was walking past, then jumped out and caught hold of her by her clothes, threw her on the ground, and cut her throat. Edward Glass asked if he had ever envied any member of the family, to which he answered 'No'.

Sarah Brock, who had previously been employed by the family as a servant, said that she believed the prisoner had 'a kind of kindness' for the younger

Sarah Glass, but she never saw him touch her nor speak to her. She testified to the handkerchief being the property of the prisoner. The next witness was John Gardiner, turnkey of the gaol, who produced a jacket which had been taken from the prisoner's back. It bore bloodstains and other marks which suggested that blood had been washed out. Constable Thomas Wood also produced some clothes which he had taken off the prisoner when Friend was first apprehended at the magistrate's house, and these also revealed bloodstains.

No case for the defence was offered. Charles Seymour confirmed that he was present when the prisoner was examined on 23 March, and produced his confession. Friend, he said, was neither threatened nor promised anything when he dictated the statement, which was read out to the court.

The judge then asked the prisoner if he had any witnesses to call or defence to make, but the answer was 'No'. The judge then recapitulated the evidence to the jury, who took merely a minute to arrive at a verdict of guilty. There was, therefore, no need to put Friend on trial for the murder of Edward Glass as well. In his summing up, the judge said that the second murder 'had been as much as possible kept out of view; but what had led the prisoner to commit these horrid murders, he could not conceive'. It gave him some satisfaction to record that Friend had conducted himself with great propriety in prison and that he had spent the time in reflection and prayer. Yet this could not mitigate the fact that the murder of Sarah Glass was one of the most malicious, premeditated and voluntary acts of atrocity he had ever come across, devoid of any redeeming features that might have given rise to some measure of regret for the prisoner concerned. There could be no hope of mercy, and the only course for the prisoner now was to apply himself to preparation by repentance and prayer for another world.

Mr Justice Burrough then passed a sentence of death. This should have been carried out on Saturday 31 March, but Burrough expressed a wish that Friend should have one last Sunday on which he could make his peace with God, so he granted him a respite until the Monday. If Friend had hopes of a more immediate end to his ordeal, he was disappointed. He seemed almost motionless as he was led from the dock.

During his final weekend in captivity, he admitted that he had originally thought of murdering Sarah Glass about a month previously, but had tried to put the thought out of his mind. He had repeatedly asked her to marry him and it was her persistent refusal, rather than jealousy of her relationship with any other man, that had driven him to kill. It was obviously not a crime committed on the spur of the moment.

A large crowd was present as he went to the Exeter gallows at midday on 2 April 1827. In accordance with the usual procedure, his body was sent to the local surgeons for dissection after being cut down.

# 7

# 'BY THE LORD'S MERCY YOU'LL HANG ME INNOCENT!'

*Exeter, 1829*

In September 1820 Samuel Westcombe married Kerziah Brown at St Sidwell's Church, Exeter. He was about thirty-six years old and his bride thirteen years younger. They settled in a house at Whipton in the Exeter parish of Heavitree. Throughout the area he was known as a cheerful hardworking man, in good health if a little on the stout side. Kerziah was said to be rather eccentric, and when they took in a lodger, Richard Quaintance,

*St Sidwell's Church, Exeter, c. 1830.*

himself a married man with a family, she was thought to be on rather too familiar terms with the man.

Samuel's workmate, Robert Broom, spent much of Tuesday 5 May 1829 helping him to prepare a hedge. They started work at around 6.30 a.m, barely stopping until the job was finished nearly twelve hours later. Samuel seemed in the best of spirits, and Broom had no idea that it was the last time he would ever see him. On the following night Westcombe died in his bed.

Shortly before midnight on 6 May, Kerziah called some neighbours round to the house, presumably to help lay Samuel out for the undertaker. If this was her intention, it was a strange thing to do. When they came round they found the body very cold and stiff, and thought he might have been dead for up to twenty-four hours. In view of Kerziah Westcombe's odd reputation, they alerted the authorities, who decided to hold an inquest.

The coroner's jury met from 1 p.m. on 8 May until 3 a.m. the following day. An autopsy revealed traces of poison in the stomach, which was sent for further analysis. Tests revealed that arsenic was present, and in sufficient quantities to kill Samuel. As a result Mrs Westcombe and Quaintance were held in custody on suspicion of murder.

An Exeter druggist, William Salter, came forward to vouch for having sold 3 ounces of arsenic for *6d* to Mr Quaintance, who was sometimes known by the first name Frank rather than Richard, and to two other men. They had visited him about three weeks earlier. Joseph Hodge and William Collis had both been at Exeter Quay when Quaintance asked them to accompany him to the shop, after he had initially been refused the arsenic unless it was sold in the presence of witnesses. He had claimed he needed it to kill rats for his master, and Collis warned him that he ought to be careful when using it in case it killed anything else by accident.

Quaintance was unemployed at the time. He had applied to the Heavitree parish overseers of the poor, claiming he could find no employment, either in his preferred trade of thatching or anything else, so they had put him to work on the parish roads. At the end of April he finally succeeded in getting some thatching. When questioned about the arsenic, he said he had been asked to buy it by Samuel Westcombe, who had paid for it, and he could not be held responsible if the latter had taken any of it himself.

Samuel Westcombe's blind sister-in-law, Mary, had touched his face after he died. It struck her that the skin felt unusually soft and most unlike the bodies of her deceased children. To her, this was a sure sign of unnatural death. Something else gave her grounds for suspicion. In Heavitree she had met a group of people who were sure that her brother-in-law had been poisoned by his wife. Kerziah had long had a dubious reputation in the neighbourhood, though the main misdemeanour which the locals appear to have laid at her door was that she used to read the Lord's Prayer backwards. Some people considered this a sign of eccentricity, although in certain circles the practice was not uncommon. When Mary told Kerziah that she was sure the surgeons would open her husband's body to investigate the cause of his death, the defensive widow answered that she would rather have a sword run through her body than allow him to be opened. It seemed likely that an autopsy would be held, and she asked Mary to stay with the body on the night of Friday 8 May while she went out, perhaps because she thought someone might call in connection with the post-mortem examination. She did not return until around 5 a.m. the next day.

When she came back, she did not say where she had been. Within a few minutes she left again, this time to go to a friend's house to ask for money for bail in case she was arrested by the authorities. Before leaving, she told Mary that her husband had picked some savine, a herb popular with pregnant women who wanted to miscarry their children or ensure a stillbirth, from Mr Rew's garden. Mary thought Kerziah was trying to suggest that her husband was wicked enough to have taken the arsenic himself, in order that she, Kerziah, should be blamed for giving it to him. Kerziah had not added that she herself was in the habit of giving savine to young women in the district and had used it on herself. She had also given some to a lady's maid in order to help her retain a post which she would have lost as the result of an unwanted pregnancy.

Guyas Davey, the landlord, who slept downstairs from the Westcombes in the same room as Quaintance, recalled that on the evening before he died, Samuel Westcombe had asked for a firkin of cider, saying he was so thirsty he could drink the sea dry. Guyas's eighteen-year-old daughter Martha had seen Kerziah adding some thickening to the broth she had prepared for her husband and noticed that she did not test it afterwards. Later that evening she and Kerziah went for a walk together, during which Kerziah said she would marry no man but Knowles, a man of whom Martha had never heard before. It struck her that this was a very strange remark for a married woman to make, and Martha wondered whether Kerziah had some mystery lover – in addition to Quaintance. Mrs Davey and her other daughter, Eliza, had already asked Quaintance to leave the house because his excessive familiarity with Mrs Westcombe was starting to cause gossip in the neighbourhood, telling him he ought to return to his own wife, Mary, and their two children at their home at South Wonford, just over a mile away. Quaintance had moved into the Westcombes' house at Whipton six weeks earlier, and said that he was taking his meals with them because Mrs Davey had been too unwell to do the cooking.

On the crucial Wednesday, Quaintance had gone to work as usual for John Horrell, a thatcher, who was expecting him to put in overtime. Instead he left early, saying he was going to visit his estranged wife in Heavitree and buy some meat. On Thursday Horrell and his thirteen-year-old son William saw Quaintance and a young girl at 5.30 a.m., walking down the hill from Clyst towards Heavitree, and when they stopped to say hello to him, he said he had been out to Newton Poppleford to report a death. Horrell wondered at first whether Kerziah must have passed away suddenly – her sister Abelina Bolt, who lived in Newton Poppleford, was the guardian of Abelina, Kerziah's daughter from an early liaison before her marriage to Samuel Westcombe. Quaintance then told Horrell that it was Sam 'Stuggs', his nickname for Westcombe, who had just died. He seemed unduly keen to know if a wife was entitled to withhold permission to have her husband's body opened, and whether a doctor could override her wishes and have such a thing done regardless.

When he reported for work later that day, Quaintance seemed completely exhausted and fell asleep at one point. As he had walked a considerable distance the previous day, for reasons which were never fully revealed but seemed rather suspicious, it was hardly surprising.

At the Summer Assizes the courtroom was full to witness the trial of Kerziah Westcombe and Richard Quaintance for the murder of Samuel Westcombe. Quaintance was also charged with maliciously inciting Kerziah to kill her husband. In accordance with its usual practice, *The Times* seemed all too ready to judge the prisoners on physical appearance alone. Mrs Westcombe, the reporter noted, was

> an ill-favoured person, of upwards of 35 years of age, with sunken eyes, cocked nose, high cheek-bones, and a mouth like a gash across the face. The expression of her features is as bad as their conformation. Her figure possesses no points of attraction; the shoulders are high and the breasts flat. Altogether Kezia Wescombe* is an extremely coarse and repulsive-looking person.

Quaintance cut an equally unprepossessing figure:

> his appearance is more favourable than that of the female prisoner; there is no expression of ferocity in his face, which is better formed than that of his paramour. He has a long and rather straight nose, and his eyes, which are rather small in proportion to his other features, look dimly forth from beneath over-arching brows. More stupid-looking faces we have seen, but few more indicative of weakness and prostration of intellect.

At the beginning of the proceedings, Kerziah listened carefully to everything that was said, and continually shook her head or muttered under her breath

---

* Reports of the case in *The Times* spell the surname as Wescombe and the prisoner's Christian name as Kezia. I have preferred the variation used in local sources instead.

while the witnesses for the prosecution were speaking. From time to time she would talk to herself when irritated by some of the testimony brought against her, or she would address her companion at the bar, whom she appeared to be inciting once or twice to cross-examine the witnesses.

While much of the evidence against them was circumstantial, the pair's chances of acquittal lay in a case for the defence put together by Kerziah's solicitor, F. Coleridge. It made the most of Samuel Westcombe's depressive moods. For these, the prosecution averred, his wife's unpleasant behaviour towards him had been largely responsible.

Mary Richards, a married daughter of the landlord of the house, was called to tell the jury that some sixteen months previously, long before Kerziah met Quaintance, Mr Westcombe had threatened to take his own life because of his wife's infidelity. She also told the court that he had been so angry with his wife that he had beaten her, and she left the house for a fortnight, before he persuaded her to return. When Eliza Davey said that she and her mother had advised Quaintance to leave the house, Kerziah's counsel for the defence, Mr Frazer, objected on the grounds that the prisoners were on trial for murder, and this constituted an attempt to raise a collateral issue, making out by implication a charge of adultery against them as well. Mr Justice Burrough countered this by ruling that anything which 'tended to show a connexion and mutual understanding subsisting between the prisoners, might be received as evidence against them'. Frazer continued to argue that, not content with proving that the parties were together, the prosecution counsel were going beyond this, and attempting to prove a distinct charge of adultery. Yet the judge still insisted that the evidence was admissible in the circumstances.

On the Wednesday night, the deceased had returned from work and asked if he could have potatoes for his tea. As there were none in the house, his wife had made the broth for him before going on her walk with her neighbour Martha Davey. This walk, it was suggested, had probably been timed to give her an alibi for the murder, as it would show that a sufficient period elapsed for Samuel to kill himself. When Kerziah and Martha returned to the house, he complained of a thirst and cold tremors. He asked his wife to rub his legs, which had become very cold, but she refused. Eleanor Jarman, an elderly widow who lived in the next room, heard him call out at about 8.45, 'Lord have mercy on me, what pain I am in!' After that all was quiet until Kerziah appeared with the neighbours at about midnight, having claimed that her husband had been dead for ten minutes. They soon decided that it was probably more like three hours.

Two witnesses came forward to say that they had frequently heard Samuel Westcombe threaten to kill himself, and he did not give the impression of being a happy man. It was quite likely that he had taken his own life, they said. However, the weight of evidence against the prisoners was so over-whelming that after Mr Justice Burrough had spent about ninety minutes summing up the case, it only took six minutes for the jury to return a verdict of guilty against both.

Kerziah took it particularly badly. At the start of the trial she paid close attention to every word being said in the courtroom, claimed that the evidence being given against them was all lies, and gave the impression that she was confident that they would be acquitted. During the latter stages, she looked increasingly unsure of herself. A chair was provided for her and she sat down, looking ever more resigned. But when the verdict was given she appeared defiant, shouting out loudly that she knew nothing about the poison until she was arrested. Mr Justice Burrough sentenced them both to be hanged on Monday next and their bodies given to the surgeons for dissection. 'By the Lord's mercy you'll hang me innocent!' she called out. By contrast, Quaintance showed no emotion.

Soon, however, Kerziah saw there was no point in trying to evade the truth any longer. She showed some remorse as she admitted her guilt, confessing that they had divided the arsenic Quaintance had bought on a pair of bellows, mixed into two equal portions for their respective spouses. He had mixed small amounts with his wife's tea, but when she tasted it she found it so awful that she refrained from taking another sip. Their young daughter had asked to finish it, but Quaintance threw the rest into the fireplace. On Tuesday 4 May they had decided to do away with Samuel Westcombe by putting some of the arsenic into his salt cellar and more into the thickening of the broth he was given. Quaintance made a confession along similar lines and gave the impression that he was not very intelligent.

On Sunday 16 August 1829 Quaintance's daughters, Mary and Ann, aged eleven and eight respectively, were taken by their brother to pay their father a last visit in the gaol at Exeter. Their mother was still too unwell from the effects of the arsenic to join them. That same day Kerziah was visited by her brother and three sisters. After these farewells, the prisoners were led to the chapel for divine service, where the Revd E. Chave gave a sermon based on a text from the gospel of St Luke, Chapter 12: 'Be not afraid of them that kill the body, and after that have no more that they can do. But I will forewarn you whom ye shall fear: fear Him which, after he hath killed, hath power to cast into hell; yea, I say unto you, fear Him.'

A rumour that the execution was to be delayed in view of Kerziah's supposed pregnancy proved to be without foundation, and the hanging was fixed for Monday 17 August. Quaintance was led to the press-room, wearing his usual working clothes, crying aloud like a small child. He 'repeatedly called for mercy from on high'. Kerziah was barefoot and wore a long loose cloak over white trousers drawn in at the ankles. Her face was filled with horror and she had to be supported the whole time because she was close to fainting. Quaintance had asked for his hands not to be bound until he had said his last farewell to her. As she entered the room, she fell back into the arms of those supporting her, so he shuffled across to her as well as his leg irons would permit.

When Quaintance was asked if he wanted anything else, he said he wanted Mrs Westcombe 'for God's sake to shake hands with him'. As she gave him her hand, she said, 'I am angry with you though, 'tis you that brought me to this.' 'Don't say that,' he answered, 'it was you that brought it upon me.' Tears rolled down his cheeks as he continued, 'My dear soul, don't say so.' Kerziah retorted, 'You brought it upon yourself. I find no fault in you, nor should you in me, we are both guilty alike.' His last words to her were, 'I hope we shall meet again', to which she replied, 'In Heaven'.

As the hangman pinioned her arms, she begged him not to cut them off. She was carried to the scaffold, where Quaintance was already waiting, and placed in a chair as the rope was adjusted around her neck. When asked if they had anything further to say, he said he had nothing to add, while she was unable to speak, faced with a crowd of around 15,000. The hangman advised her to stand, but she was unable to do so without the support of three men.

After they were hanged, Kerziah's body was sent to the Devon & Exeter Hospital for dissection. The judge had relented in Quaintance's case and he rescinded his previous order, now allowing his corpse to be given to his brother for burial. Though they were hardly worthy of heroic status, a print of the executed prisoners was reproduced and offered for sale, while a local craftsman, Mr Dean, made an exact model of the Westcombes' home and exhibited it at Exeter Castle, with all proceeds being sent to Quaintance's widow.

# 8

# THE MURDERER AND THE BOOK OF POETRY

Few murderers can have been immortalised in such a peculiar fashion as George Cudmore. Born in Iddesleigh in about 1800, he had had a number of farm labouring jobs by the time he married Grace Martin, eight years older than him, at Dolton parish church. She had been born and brought up at Dolton, but the overseers of the poor did not want him in the parish, so they decided to send him somewhere else. After checking his employment history they established that he had previously worked at Roborough for a while, so they sent him there.

The Cudmores settled together at Roborough in September 1822, but they were not generally liked. In March 1823 the cider cellar of Emmanuel Hockaday, a well-known and respected resident of the town, was broken into. Cudmore was charged with breaking and entering, though at the Exeter Summer Assizes he was acquitted because of lack of evidence.

The couple had four children: Mary, born 1824, William the following year (he died at the age of four months), Thomas a year later, and finally George in 1829. By the time of George's birth, the pair had become estranged. They had taken in a lodger, Sarah Dunn, and George was having an affair with her. He and Grace regularly quarrelled, and after one row George told her that soon she would 'never see his face again'.

On Monday 13 October 1829 Grace paid a call on their neighbour, Jane Trigger, and complained of a heavy cold. During the next few days she became seriously ill with headaches, a burning pain in her stomach and side, general nausea and loose teeth. George seemed very concerned and sent for Dr Owen, who bled her and diagnosed pleurisy. His apprentice, William Risdon, prescribed laxative powders, but she complained that they had a peculiar taste, and also said that the elder blossom tea her husband was giving her made her very sick. Trigger had no reason to suspect that George was not doing all he reasonably could, and seemed unconcerned by the fact that Cudmore and the lodger, who were apparently lovers, were jointly looking after a sick woman whose death might well be in their best interests.

By Friday Grace was much worse. Dr Owen was sent for again and further powders to prevent vomiting were prescribed. But she continued to deteriorate, and on the Sunday morning she told Trigger that she felt so ill she did not expect she would live long enough to go downstairs again. In the evening she said wearily that she would never speak to Trigger again and did not expect to survive until the morning, as she was sure her husband was trying to destroy her. At 1 a.m. on 20 October 1829 she died. Later that morning Jane Trigger arrived to find George wiping his eyes with a handkerchief, bewailing the death of his wife. Sarah Dunn, the lodger, and two other ladies whose job it was to lay out the body were present in the cottage at the time.

A couple of days later Grace was buried in the churchyard at Roborough. Rumours about the cause of her death were multiplying and some of the parishioners were sure she had been helped on her way. A decision was taken to exhume the body. The overseer of the poor, William Downe, had known Grace since she was a girl, and he was present when the coffin was opened the following week. Although there had been a degree of external decomposition, he could still recognise her features. Alexander Pidler, a surgeon from Torrington, had been called to dissect the body. Grace's stomach and intestines were much inflamed, their appearance being consistent with arsenic poisoning. Dr Owen was asked for his opinion. In the stomach he found coffee-coloured liquid with a white substance floating on it. A surgeon from Exeter, Mr Pridham, analysed the substances and agreed that arsenic was present.

When the Cudmores' house was searched, Mr Downe found a paper wrapper marked 'Poison' concealed in the thatch over a window. George Cudmore and Sarah Dunn were arrested and charged with murder. Dunn made a confession to Mr Kingdon, the magistrates' clerk at Torrington, telling him that Mr Cudmore had told her that he planned to boil a dose for his wife. She had warned him not to, as if he did he would surely be hanged for it. She also said that he had put poison in his wife's tea. Cudmore was ready to blame Dunn, saying that she had given him the idea at harvest time when they were in the fields. He said she had suggested that in return for some 'trade' she would take responsibility for doing away with his wife. He also said that Dunn had looked after the poison and threatened that if he did not eliminate his wife, she would take it herself.

The couple were kept in custody at the house of Constable William Thomas, to whom Cudmore confessed at length that he was responsible. His wife, he said, had asked him to boil something for a sweat and he mixed up some elder blossom and agrimony for the purpose. He had some arsenic in a white cloth and he boiled them together. When it was done he took some to his wife and had some himself, being very sick afterwards as a result.

That night Cudmore asked Dunn for her forgiveness. When she said that she forgave him, he told her that he would never have killed his wife had it not been for her. She agreed she was as bad as him and that they both deserved the same punishment for their sins.

When they were put on trial at the Spring Assizes on 23 March 1830, Sarah Dunn had nothing to say in her defence. George Cudmore gave a detailed statement to the court, taking about forty-five minutes. He said that the arsenic found in the thatch had been bought two years earlier for killing rats. He had never shown anything but the greatest concern for his wife's health and had regularly consulted the doctor. After her death, he said, he had asked to have her body opened in order to allay suspicions in the neighbourhood that he had poisoned her.

The jury were asked to consider the possibility that Grace Cudmore might have taken the arsenic herself in a mood of depression at the state of her marriage, or alternatively that she had been unlawfully murdered by her husband with Sarah Dunn as an accessory. It took them fifteen minutes to find him guilty, but not his lodger. As the judge prepared to pass sentence, he asked the prisoner if there was any reason why he should not be executed. Cudmore protested his innocence, but in vain.

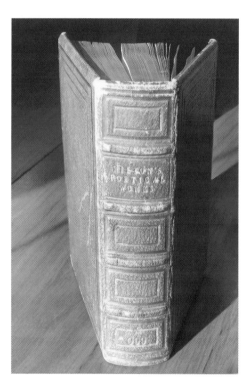

*The works of John Milton, 1850, bound in skin taken from the corpse of George Cudmore.* (Westcountry Studies Library)

Two days later he went to the gallows. While he admitted that he accepted the justice of his sentence, he continued to maintain that Sarah Dunn had administered the poison. She was in the crowd who had come to see him hanged, and as the executioner completed his task she gave a loud shriek. Later that year she gave birth to an illegitimate child, her fourth, though it was not known whether Cudmore was the father.

His body was sent to the Devon & Exeter Hospital for dissection. To this day, the Westcountry Studies Library in Exeter retains a copy of *The Works of John Milton*, published in 1850, bound in his skin. A local surgeon carefully removed the skin from the flesh and kept it rolled up for twenty years before somebody – maybe the surgeon himself – thought of using it for this purpose.

# 9

# AN INFANTICIDE

*Plymouth, 1832*

The ruthless disposal of illegitimate children was all too prevalent in the nineteenth century (see also pp. 57–65). One of those who paid the price was Mary Kellaway, an unmarried woman of twenty-eight from Stowford. At an early age she had been seduced by a man who promised to marry her, but he abandoned her when she was carrying his child, who was now living with relatives. Having lost her self-respect once, she then had another affair and another child outside wedlock, which died, though whether of natural causes is not known.

Finding herself in an interesting condition without a wedding ring on her finger for the third time, she was determined to conceal her situation from her family and moved from her home to lodgings in Devonport for the birth. On 12 November 1831 she gave birth to a daughter in a room she shared with Mary Thomas, a sailor's wife, at 20 Dockwall. Thomas had only arrived to share lodgings with her about a week before, and the women shared a bed, except at weekends when Thomas slept on board her husband's ship in Plymouth Sound.

Mary Thomas was aware that her co-lodger was expecting a child – as they shared a bed it would have been impossible for her to be ignorant of the fact. On the night that the birth occurred, the only sounds she heard – as she testified subsequently in court – were of Mary Kellaway getting in and out of bed a couple of times during the hours of darkness. When she got up in the morning, she saw three spots of blood on a rather wet floor at the foot of the bed, one spot much larger than the others. When she asked about it, Kellaway said she had spilt some water. Later, Kellaway tried to remove some more blood from the floor, claiming it was from a cut.

As Kellaway was evidently no longer pregnant, it was decided that the premises would have to be searched. The landlady, Mrs MacDonald, soon found the infant, wrapped in a quilt. She fetched some scissors to cut the string around it, but Kellaway snatched them out of her hand and turned quickly to the baby, trying to cut the cord around his neck. Suddenly aware of what Kellaway was doing, Mrs MacDonald shouted, 'By God, she has murdered her child!'

When she was apprehended for the crime, Kellaway admitted at once that her room-mate had had nothing to do with the murder. Assuming the baby would not live, she had had no linen or clothes for it and, when questioned about this, said she did not realise she was coming to the end of her full term.

When the case came to trial at Exeter Assizes in March 1832, Mr Bone, the coroner, said that the prisoner greatly regretted the baby's death because she loved children very much. The idea of killing the child only occurred to her because she saw a chance to end her shame. She did it on the spur of the moment.

The trial lasted about five hours, much of it punctuated by the sobs of the prisoner. Though allowances were made for her, the evidence of Mr W.P. Mould, the parish surgeon, that the child had been born alive, was enough to convince the jury. They returned a verdict of guilty, adding a rider that mercy should be extended to the prisoner if it was within Mr Justice Gaseler's power to do so. He had other ideas, and in passing the death sentence, spoke of the need for parents to protect their own children, saying that mercy could not be offered to Kellaway because it was beyond doubt that she was guilty of a revolting crime.

While awaiting execution at Exeter gaol, she had a visit from her father, a labourer, who walked the 35 miles from Stowford. She was also visited by her married sister. A number of 'benevolent ladies', it was recorded, also came to console her. Mr Cole, the governor, took pity on her and moved her from the part of the prison where the more hardened inmates were kept to a more suitable wing.

At the end she confessed her guilt, accepting the just nature of her punishment. The murder of her child had not been a premeditated act, she said, but she had been caught unawares during the night, and decided there and then to do away with her baby. She went to the gallows shortly after midday on 26 March 1832, her last request being to Mr Cole, asking that he should try and make sure that her surviving child would be looked after well. A reporter from *The Times* was most unimpressed by the spectacle surrounding her death, noting that large crowds of people, many well-dressed, 'were seen hastening with careless indifference towards the scene of execution, and of these the major part were women, many of them abandoned creatures certainly, but a portion of them respectable wives and mothers. We trust the females of Exeter will never again so far degrade themselves as those who attended this spectacle of death did so on the present occasion.'

# 10

# DEATH
# AFTER THE FAIR

## *Moretonhampstead, 1835*

Jonathan May of Sowton Barton, Dunsford, was a well-to-do farmer in his late forties. Although a bachelor, he was believed to be courting a lady from Tiverton. Maybe he planned to settle down a little later in life than his contemporaries, not just for the benefits of family life but also to have children who would inherit the farm after him. In the community he was widely respected, though he had a reputation as a harsh employer with high standards. At least one of his men discovered this to his cost.

In 1834 George Avery, a well-built young man who supplemented his wages by taking part in occasional wrestling matches, was sent by the farmer to collect some logs from an outlying woodpile and deliver them to his house. May then set off for Exeter, but for some reason he turned back – only to find Avery unloading wood from the wagon not at the farm, but instead at the tied cottage in which May had allowed him to live. He was promptly sacked and May said he would give him no references in future; moreover, he would ensure that everyone knew of his dishonesty, so he would be unlikely to find work. Avery vowed he would get even and then left the area, determined to make his living as a wrestler.

Thursday 16 July 1835 was the day of the annual fair at Moreton-hampstead. The town had a flourishing wool trade, and the fair attracted people from near and far. May was there, hoping to get a good price for his livestock. The fair had a variety of stalls for home-made goods and sideshows, including wrestlers, fortune-tellers and other entertainers. It was one of the most important local events of the year, and a magnet for low-lifes from the neighbourhood and other parts of the country, who tended to travel from one fair to another. Among the less desirable elements present were Avery, his girlfriend Elizabeth Harris and possibly a couple of friends they had just made, whom they knew as Oliver and Turpin.

May sold about £80 worth of animals, then visited Thomas White, a tanner who lived on the corner of the square, to collect payment for oak bark used for tanning. His next stop was George Norrish, a shoemaker to whom he owed money for boots and repairs. Afterwards he returned to the White Hart, where he had left his horse. Full of good ale at the end of a good day, he was

*The White Hart, Moretonhampstead.* (© Dr Ian Mortimer)

tempted to hold forth a little less than wisely about his profits, and displayed his money to prove his point that he was 'a moderately warm man' – in other words, a success and not ashamed of it.

It was probably some time after witnessing this display of wealth by his former employer that Avery returned to his lodgings, telling his companions he was tired. As he came in through the door, he asked them what the time was and they replied that it was 8 p.m. Going upstairs to bed, he rested briefly, then came back down and asked them the time again. One of the household remarked that it was odd he should be doing this repeatedly, especially as there was a clock on the wall in front of him.

Meanwhile, merrymaking continued in Moretonhampstead, with bands playing, crowds dancing in the streets, and much cider, ale and spirits flowing. At about 10 p.m. May left on horseback to return to his farm. On his way he rode slowly through the tollgate and spoke to James Nosworthy, the toll-keeper, bidding him goodnight.

At about midnight Nicholas Taverner and his wife Grace, and her brother John Tallamy and his wife, set out to go home to Harcot. They were taking a

*The Rectory, Moretonhampstead.* (© Dr Ian Mortimer)

short-cut home down Shute Lane, a track near Jacob's Well, a natural spring where a horses' drinking trough was to be found. At the top of the lane they found a horse wandering around beside the hedge. Nicholas took it back to the town, and only then did he realise that it belonged to Jonathan May. Suspecting an accident or something worse, he headed back along the main Exeter road where he found May lying unconscious on his back in a pool of blood, his pockets turned out and his waistcoat undone. He shouted 'Murder!' and his wife, who had stayed there waiting for her husband to return, came running over. She stayed with May while Nicholas made his way as quickly as possible to Moretonhampstead for help. He went to Dr Alfred Puddicombe's house in Cross Street, now The Old Rectory, then got a horse and cart to take the injured man back to the White Hart, where May had recently been celebrating in such good spirits. His wounds were so severe that he never regained consciousness, despite the care and attention of his surgeon, Dr John Ponsford, and he died at 9 p.m. the following day. May's assailant assumed that death would be attributed to a fall from his horse.

A receipt for 30s for some boots and shoes that had been given to May on the evening of his death by George Norrish was missing from his coat. It was found in his pocket-book in a field at Hennock, a few miles away, some months later. Two £5 notes were still in a pocket on the inside of his waistcoat, although his watch could not be found. At the scene of the crime a local thatcher, Henry Luscombe, found a broken blood-covered stick 3 feet long, cut from an ash tree, and this was assumed to be the murder weapon. Another part of the stick was found in a nearby ditch by William Bracknell, a stonemason, along with a piece of blood-soaked material from a shirt frill. Blood was also spattered on the leaves of a hedge, and it seemed that May had managed to crawl on his hands and knees about 50 feet from where he first fell after being attacked.

A post-mortem was carried out by Dr Ponsford and his Moretonhampstead colleague, Dr Alfred Puddicombe. As there was very little gravel in any of the wounds, they ruled out any possibility that May had fallen and been dragged along the road by his horse. The wounds must have been caused either by kicks or by blows from a stick, though Ponsford conceded that a wound on the temple might have been caused by a kick from a horse. A coroner's inquest returned a verdict of wilful murder on 21 July, and May was buried in the churchyard at Dunsford. His gravestone bore the inscription, 'Erected to the memory of Jonathan May of Sowton Barton in this parish who was murdered as he was returning from Moreton fair about ten o'clock on the evening of 16th July A.D. 1835. Aged 48 years.'

A local solicitor, Moses Woolland Harvey, had seen the site of the struggle and the bloodstains in the hedge and on the road. He had also noticed the tracks of two men across the adjacent barley field, leading towards Crammer's Brook, where May's pocket-book was later found by labourers William Crocker and William Caseley. In the absence of any effective police operation in the area, he took up the case in an effort to apprehend the culprits – he assumed that at least two people must be responsible for the murder. Harvey and May's brothers, Walter and John, jointly offered a reward of £100 for any information leading to conviction of the guilty party. A free pardon was offered to anyone who confessed to being an accomplice, on condition that they had not been directly involved in the murder. Harvey was regarded by less law-abiding elements as a dangerous man and a tiresome busybody who would not rest until he had somebody in the dock, and he took to carrying a pistol for his protection. One day it went off in his pocket, wounding him in the thigh.

Suspicion immediately fell on Avery, whose dismissal by the farmer and subsequent threats against him were no secret. He and his girlfriend Elizabeth Harris, who had been travelling around the country with him for the previous few months, were taken into custody at Exeter, but released when Avery managed to prove that he was in his lodgings on the night May was killed.

*The gravestone of
Jonathan May,
Dunsford Church.
(© Dr Ian Mortimer)*

George Avery had been arrested on a charge of murder some months before, but he was discharged owing to a lack of evidence and the corroboration of his witnesses. He was later detained on a separate charge of assaulting a Dunsford labourer at Alphington in the spring of 1835, sentenced to death, but reprieved and sentenced to transportation instead. Within a few days he became the ringleader in a plan to escape from the gaol.

In the summer of 1836 Thomas Oliver was in Dorchester gaol, awaiting trial on a charge of robbery with violence. While exercising with other inmates in the yard, he boasted that the biggest job he had ever done was when he and 'Turpin' had knocked a Devonshire farmer on the head and robbed him. This reached the ears of the prison chaplain, who knew of the May murder, and he wrote to Harvey. The latter decided to pay a special visit to Dorchester, where he found the watch and various other articles belonging to May in the prisoner's lodgings. These proved sufficient to incriminate him.

Edmund Galley, a brickmaker, was well known around fairs in the south-east of England as a rogue and he was nicknamed Dick Turpin, after the notorious highwayman. A description of him was widely circulated, and although he lay low for a while, he was apprehended when Thomas McGill, a London police sergeant, went to Coldbath Fields gaol to interview him while he was being held there on a charge of vagrancy. Galley told him he had been born at Kingston-upon-Thames and claimed he had never been in Devon. He said he was at the races in Reigate when the murder took place, but later he changed his story to say he was at Dartford, working at the Windmill public house. The police ignored his second statement. His supposed employer, Mr Rowe, had no recollection of Galley's working for him, and it turned out that Galley had only been employed casually by the carpenter for beer money.

At the expiry of his sentence for vagrancy on 30 April, Galley was arrested by McGill and taken to Bow Street, where he saw a handbill on the walls giving details of May's murder. He then realised that this must be the reason for his arrest. Shortly after his arrival in Exeter, Elizabeth Harris was brought in to identify him. She had described him as being well built with bushy whiskers, and at first she thought this puny-looking whiskerless man was somebody different. Gradually she reached the decision that although he was 'strangely altered', he must be the one. Others came forward to say that they had seen both Oliver and Galley in the area at the time of the murder, and swore that Galley was the man they had seen with Oliver at Moreton-hampstead the previous year.

Edmund Galley and Thomas Oliver, whose real name was Thomas Infield but who was generally known as Buckingham Joe, were charged with the murder. The case came to trial before Mr Justice Williams at the Crown Court, Exeter, on 28 July 1836. The judge was already notorious for having ordered a sentence of transportation on the 'Tolpuddle Martyrs' two years earlier for forming a trade union in Dorset.

The greatest stir in the courtroom occurred when Harris came to give evidence for the prosecution. She claimed to have been at Moretonhampstead on the eve of the fair and to have seen the prisoners entering the Bell Inn together on the following afternoon. She knew them by sight as she had seen them at earlier fairs at Bromhill, near Taunton, and at Dorchester and Weymouth. She also claimed to have heard them talking in travellers' slang. Buckingham said to Turpin, 'It's a fine-looking gaff, and there's some crusty looking blocks in it, and we must have some gilt in the rot.' Elizabeth thought this meant that it was a large fair with some wealthy-looking farmers present, and that they were planning to rob some of them that very evening.

She said she had had an argument with her lover after tea, and she set off to try and cadge a lift on a cart out of Moretonhampstead at about 10 p.m., but could not catch up with it so she turned back. The two prisoners passed her on the road outside the town where there was a steep hill and a sharp bend. She had stopped to loosen her bootlace, and heard somebody say goodnight to the turnpike gatekeeper shortly before May rode into view. Recalling what the two men had been saying, she turned and followed May from a distance, and as he reached the top of the hill by the milestone, she said that she saw Oliver leap from the hedge and grab his horse by the head.

'You're just going home, farmer', was what she thought she heard him say. 'I am,' replied May. At this point, Turpin emerged from the shadows behind the farmer, carrying a stick. He struck May on the left side of the head with two blows, but the farmer stayed on his horse until Oliver dragged him on to the ground. They fought for about five minutes, Turpin continuing to hit May. 'If you rob me, for God's sake don't take my life' were his last words before Turpin kicked him hard twice and he lost consciousness. Both men climbed over a gate into a cornfield with a pocket-book and what looked like either a watch or a seal for fastening letters. Elizabeth said she was too scared to move, and stood still in the shadow of the hedge for what seemed a very long time, then went back to George Avery's house at Moretonhampstead.

At 6 next morning at the lodging house of Mary Splatt Elizabeth was taken into custody on suspicion of murder along with several of her travelling companions, including Avery, 'Black Soph' (Elizabeth Weeks), Andrew Carpenter, who was kept in custody for nine months and then released as he

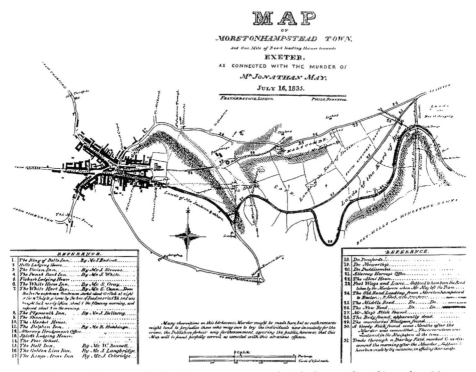

*Map of Moretonhampstead, showing areas connected with the murder of Jonathan May, 1835. (Moretonhampstead History Society)*

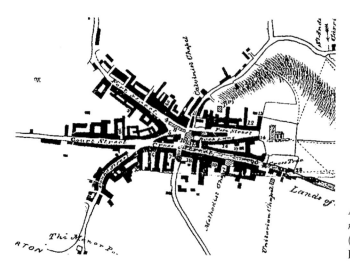

*An enlargement of the map of the main street.* (Moretonhampstead History Society)

was dying, and Arthur Pardew. Elizabeth Harris spent a month in prison at Exeter before being released to spend some time with her sister in Taunton. Four months later she was arrested again, tried and sentenced for a theft in North Devon. On that occasion, in February 1836, she told Tryphoena Lampen, the Matron Turnkey of Exeter Bridewell, that she had witnessed the murder of Jonathan May. She claimed she had not even told George Avery what she had seen, and that she did not expect nor ask for a pardon in return for giving evidence against the prisoners.

In court Galley directed his questions to her in some disbelief. 'Can you look at me with a clear conscience,' he asked her, 'and say you saw me do what you say to this man?' She replied, 'I did, and you know that I did, by what I have told you since.'

'Did you ever see me in company with this man,' he asked again, pointing to Oliver, 'till you see me in gaol?' 'Yes, at Bromhill Fair.' Galley asserted that she had never seen him there, nor anywhere in Devonshire before. 'I did, and at Bridgwater Fair together,' she said. Galley turned to the judge. 'My Lord, she mistakes me for another man, I never was in Devonshire in my life, till I was brought to the prison; I know I am not the man my Lord, and God Almighty knows I am not the man; she swears in the name they have given me my Lord, and not my body.' Elizabeth insisted that he was the man. 'If you know me to be the man,' he asked, 'why did you not mention this before?' 'Because I am afraid if I am out, but I am not afraid when I am in there,' she said, meaning the gaol. 'I think you should be glad I have told of it, as I'm sure you can have no peace nor rest on account of it. I had not.'

Galley was highly suspicious of Harris's motives, as he pointed out to the judge. He told the latter that 'she might get her freedom, she swears my life away. I know I am not the man, and God Almighty knows it. I am not the person who did this, thanks be to God. I was brought down to Exeter on the

1st May last, and never was in the county in all my life before. I never saw that woman in all my life, my Lord, till I saw her in the gaol.' The judge asked Harris if she had any doubt that these were the men she saw commit the murder. She assured him that she had none. Turpin was definitely the man who came out of the hedge and passed behind the farmer towards the left side of the horse. He was the one who struck the blow with the stick, she said.

Two local residents, Ann Carpenter and her daughter Jane, recalled staying at a boarding house in Butchers Row, Exeter, on 13 July. They thought they saw the two prisoners there with a woman whom they knew as 'Black Ann'. In August they saw Oliver at Wilton after the Salisbury races. He was with 'Black Ann' and Elizabeth McKinley, but all of them denied at first having been in Exeter in July. 'Black Ann' later admitted to Ann Carpenter that she had been in Exeter, but she was not with Oliver at the time. 'Black Ann' had washed Oliver's smock coat in the courtyard, but was unable to remove a suspicious-looking stain. They had a violent argument, attacked each other, and 'Black Ann' ended up with a nosebleed. Elizabeth McKinley remarked loudly, so that Oliver could hear, that the stain must have been the blood of Jonathan May. The coat was produced in court and a rusty-coloured stain was still visible. Oliver said he had already been convicted because the mark had been taken as evidence.

Catherine Gaffrey, Mary Smith and Mary Marengo all testified in court that the prisoners before them at the assizes were the same men who had stayed at Mrs Marengo's house the previous July, though Gaffrey retracted her statement after the trial. The two men had been studying a booklet giving dates of the local fairs and decided they would go to Moretonhampstead, but did not appear concerned that they were unlikely to arrive before it was dark. They paid for their lodgings with a gold ring and a silver snuffbox.

A lace-seller, Charlotte Clarke, said she saw two men with 'Black Ann' at the Lamb Inn on the road from Exeter to Moretonhampstead. One of them she knew to be Buckingham Joe and the other one she recognised as Turpin, who had previously tried to persuade her to buy a gold ring at Taunton. She was sure that this Turpin was not the man now facing her across the courtroom. The man she saw at the Lamb Inn had a full set of teeth – Galley had two upper teeth missing – and his dark whiskers met at the chin. He was quite respectable-looking compared to the man she now saw in court who had just served a sentence for vagrancy.

Charlotte Clarke recalled leaving the inn at the same time as the two men and 'Black Ann' at midday on the opening day of the Moretonhampstead Fair. She reached the town in the early hours of the evening, but the other three had stopped to rest about 2 miles away and she had not seen them since. She was positive that Oliver was Buckingham Joe and that he was on the Exeter Road at around the time of the murder. The landlady of the Lamb Inn felt that Galley was the other man, as did other witnesses who claimed they had seen the two robbers in Moretonhampstead during the fair. Betty Croot said she had seen him in the White Hart Inn, playing a pub game with the local apprentices and doing rather well financially in the process.

John Hiscox, a convicted thief, was serving a sentence at Dorchester gaol in September 1835. He told the court that his fellow-prisoner, Oliver, had often boasted how he and a man named Turpin had robbed a Moretonhampstead farmer before heading back through Taunton on the way to London. At the time Oliver was awaiting transportation for life for his part in three highway robberies in Dorset. Hiscox was reminded of these conversations in prison by a handbill that he was shown in the governor's office when he was being released the following January. This bill offered a reward for the capture of May's killers. At the trial Oliver was indignant about Hiscox's testimony, accusing him of 'swearing false in every word you say, and you are trying to take away my life for gain'.

At the end of the prosecution's case, Galley repeated that he was in Reigate at the time of the murder, and that the finger of suspicion had pointed at him merely because he had the misfortune to share the same nickname as one of the murderers. Had he been able to afford it, he would have obtained the services of a good lawyer who would prove his innocence beyond the shadow of a doubt. His lover, Jane Cording, had tried to obtain money from his family to help him, but only his sister was able to contribute anything – the princely sum of 5s. Mr Justice Williams had not assigned him any counsel, but had he done so, the outcome of the case might have been very different. Galley appealed to the judge: 'I am as innocent as a baby just born, and if I do suffer here through false swearing, and by persons who know nothing of me, and never saw me before, God knows that I am innocent, and I hope he will receive my soul.'

Oliver hoped that some attention would be given to Avery's comment to a fellow prisoner, William Rattenbury, who was under sentence of transportation for rum-running and assault on a coastguard officer, that Elizabeth Harris, who claimed to have witnessed the murder, had been in bed with him all night, so she could not possibly have been at Jacob's Well. Most of the information she gave about the murder could have been gleaned from the newspapers at the time, and also from her fellow rogues in prison. Avery was brought from gaol to confirm that she had been with him from just before 10 p.m. on the night of the murder, thus throwing some doubt on all her evidence. He had been meticulous in creating his own alibi at the lodgings that night, and took particular care to ask people the time throughout the evening. He was known to have sworn vengeance against May, yet he knew better than to be implicated in any physical attack on him. As he was with Oliver and Turpin at the fair, he may have had some hand in instigating the crime.

In summing up the case, Mr Justice Williams said that the jury's decision rested largely upon their opinion as to the quality of Elizabeth Harris's testimony and way of life. If the jury believed her evidence, they must convict the prisoners. He hinted that their identities had been corroborated by several of the witnesses. Significantly, he had apparently misunderstood one vital point – namely, what Charlotte Clarke had actually said when giving evidence to the effect that the man called Turpin, whom she had seen at the Lamb Inn and previously at Taunton, was definitely not the Turpin she now saw in the dock. Her words evidently had two meanings: 'this Turpin was not one of the men,' she said. She was referring to the unfortunate Galley and this should have been the main point in his defence, if only he had had any counsel to defend him.

At 9.45 p.m. the judge left the matter in the hands of the jury. Sixteen minutes later, they returned to give their verdict. Both prisoners were found guilty of murder. Galley shouted that he was innocent, and the judge paused before donning the black cap. At some length he explained to the court that the jury must have felt that the weight of Elizabeth Harris's testimony was so great that they had to convict, despite what he regarded as a suitably impartial summing up on his part. If there was any doubt, he seemed to be saying, it was not for him to decide but for the jury, thus absolving himself of responsibility in the case after the conviction had duly been given.

As he reached the part where he was about to pronounce sentence, Oliver could hold back no longer. 'My Lord,' he said, 'do not, I hope you will not, send an innocent man to the trap. The man by my side is as innocent as you are, I never saw him in my life till I saw him in gaol. I was there but this young man was not. The man who did this is known by the name of the Young Hero, or the Kentish Youth; he is also known by the name of Turpin.'

The judge replied that it was 'only on proof that we can proceed here, and we must be regulated by the evidence given. On this the jury have found you both guilty.' Oliver insisted that his partner in crime was a better-looking man than Galley, and taller. Galley continued to protest his innocence, claiming that if he had had the money, he would have been able to prove it. He could not understand why the witnesses had sworn falsely against him, and hoped God would forgive them. The judge said that if what he claimed was true, Galley must be the unhappiest man alive, a sentiment with which the prisoner must surely have agreed. He reminded them that the jury had been persuaded of his guilt and that, though human nature meant it was possible they could have been deceived, there could be no better system of justice than that under which they had been tried. He recommended that Galley should obtain his mercy and forgiveness from God in the time remaining to him, rather than from the court whose decision had been made.

Again Oliver begged the judge not to hang an innocent man, saying that all the witnesses had been deceived and mistaken in identifying a man he had never seen as his partner in Jonathan May's murder. Both men protested Galley's innocence, and the judge took several minutes before he directed that the prisoners should be taken back to the gaol to await execution without hope of mercy.

Galley had one remarkable stroke of good luck, however. During the week of the trial, a statute requiring that death sentences had to be carried out within forty-eight hours was repealed. Had this not been the case, he would have gone to the gallows then. As a result of deputations from certain well-placed people, Mr Justice Williams was persuaded that certain aspects of the case against Galley needed further investigation, and so the executions were set for Friday week.

Both men were interviewed in prison, and Oliver repeatedly swore that Galley was innocent. He also said that his partner in crime had been a man called Longley, who killed May after Oliver had pulled him from his horse. After May had been attacked, Oliver said, they both fought for the money but Longley won as he was larger and much stronger.

While awaiting execution, the deeply distressed Galley almost went to pieces. The answers he gave to the investigators were very confused at first, and he said he could not recollect where he had been on 16 July the previous year. After a day or two he calmed down, and repeated that he had been at Dartford that day. Certain details of his visit to the fair came back to him, such as an argument he had had with a man over a wager of half a crown, which led to a fight and his losing the money. He later won it back by a card trick. He named three men whom he had seen at the fair; letters were sent to them, and they replied that they all recalled seeing him there.

Thomas Oliver was hanged at Exeter gaol on 12 August 1836. He had made a strong impression on everyone at the prison with his courage, especially in his efforts to help Galley escape what he considered to be an unjust conviction. He had come to terms with his own fate. Asked at the last moment whether he had anything else to say, he said, 'All I have to say is to inform this congregation that I am a guilty man; the other is an innocent man.' Before the noose was placed around his neck, he dropped a red handkerchief, a custom which signified to the crowds that he had not betrayed his associate. He had already named Longley as the murderer, and had no reason to show him any loyalty because Longley had beaten him and taken the prize. The associate he had not implicated was probably Avery.

A few days later, a student doctor in Exeter told the prison governor that his father, a magistrate in Bath, had written to say that the Bath magistrates had remanded a man whom they believed to be Longley. They were holding him to give the Devonshire authorities a chance to take action, but they did nothing. Harvey was asked to intervene, but refused to prosecute the man, who was later released.

Galley was granted another stay of execution, until 23 September. From Exeter gaol he was taken to Woolwich and placed on the prison hulk *Ganymede*. His hair cropped and his face freshly shaven, he was placed in convict's clothes along with the other prisoners, and four key witnesses were brought to the ship to see if they could identify him. All could do so without difficulty, thus effectively proving his alibi that he was far away from Moreton-hampstead at the time of the murder. A full pardon was expected by some, but instead, because of the doubts that remained as to his innocence, the sentence was commuted to transportation for life. For two years he waited for news of his release, but in vain. In May 1839 he was sent to New South Wales on HMS *Parkfield*, and arrived there four months later.

The fact that a potentially innocent man had almost gone to the gallows added weight to the arguments of those in authority who were calling for the abolition of capital punishment in England. Judges in Devon were so mindful of the case and the possible miscarriage of justice that no executions were carried out in Exeter for another thirteen years after Oliver was hanged.

Soon after reaching Australia, Galley was given the position of overseer on a chain-gang working at Cook's River for six months. Afterwards he worked alternately as a farm servant and at his old trade of brickmaking. A campaign in England to clear his name eventually succeeded, and he was granted a Queen's Pardon in October 1879. In 1881 after a debate in the House of Commons, an agreement was made for him to be awarded compensation to let him return to England if he wished, and live out his remaining days in comfort. However, he chose to stay in New South Wales, where he had long since happily settled with his wife and children. He died peacefully in November 1885, aged about seventy.

# 11

# A GAMEKEEPER'S VIOLENT END

## Oakford Bridge, Nr Tiverton, 1839

Jacob Cottrell was an assistant gamekeeper, a married man with four young children, who lived at Oakford Bridge, near Tiverton. He was employed by Alderman Daniel. On the evening of Saturday 26 January 1839 he was called on to assist James Bowerman, the head gamekeeper, in watching the preserves, and shortly after midnight he and two others heard shooting.

Their eye soon fell on a party of three poachers – Aaron Hagley, his brother Thomas, and Matthew Maslen, whom they pursued for several miles. As they drew near Knightshayes House, the home of Mr B.B. Dickinson, one of the party left the others to call for Mr Dickinson's keeper to come and assist them, while Cottrell and another man continued the pursuit. On arriving at a field near Guddle, Maslen attacked Cottrell with a large stick.

The three poachers then walked backwards, pointing a gun at Bowerman and Cottrell. The latter followed them, and asked them their names. One of them said they were slightly drunk, and had lost their way. When the keepers asked what business they had with a gun on Sunday morning, Aaron took it from Thomas Hagley's hands, saying he would 'be damned if he [Cottrell] would not blow our brains out if we did not keep off'. No sooner had he made his threat than he fired. The bullet went through Cottrell's left cheek, eye and brain, killing him instantly.

On the following morning, Cottrell's companions identified the killer as Aaron Hagley from Loxbeare. He and his companions were arrested and charged with murder at Exeter Assizes before Mr Justice Baron Maule on 22 March, with Mr Bere and Mr Cockburn conducting the case for the prosecution, and Mr Greenwood for the defence.

Bowerman was the first to give evidence. He described meeting the men, giving chase, and being struck on the head first by Maslen, though it was only a slight tap. Other witnesses followed, including John Winter and James Venn, the other two men in the party that night. They all corroborated Bowerman's statement.

A surgeon, Robert MacDonald, confirmed that he had been called to see the body, and said that a gunshot wound had destroyed the left eye and caused the man's death. Then, a number of witnesses were called to confirm that the body was that of Cottrell, but nobody present would do so. It is unclear why neither Bowerman nor Daniel, who could easily have verified the fact, were not asked to give evidence on this. One must suppose that the judge would only accept testimony from a witness who could be regarded as more impartial; and that no impartial witnesses were prepared to cooperate suggests they were perhaps afraid of reprisals from the prisoners' associates. The defence counsel, Mr Greenwood, argued that there was a gap in the evidence as regards the identification of the body, which was necessary in order to convict the prisoners. Despite MacDonald's testimony, he also said there was no proof that Cottrell had died from a gunshot wound.

After further discussion, Mr Baron Maule said he thought that there was sufficient evidence to go to the jury, on the grounds that the man who was fired at appeared to have fallen down and that his face was covered with blood. The jury might infer that he was struck by some substance which caused his death. It was not necessary, however, either to prove that it was leaden shot or bullets, or to show that the wound was in the eye. With respect to the identification of the body, his impression was that there was not enough evidence, the only proof of this point being that the body was left in the courtyard, and that on the same day a body had been examined by the medical man. He did not think the body was adequately 'traced', and therefore it would be safer to direct the jury not to take the surgeon's evidence at all.

This made it easy for Greenwood to contend that Bowerman might not have been aware of any circumstances which could have led to the death of 'the party'. There was nothing to prove that the act was done of malice aforethought. The circumstances would induce the jury to imagine that Cottrell's death must have resulted from 'sudden irritation', such as a seizure, and the learned counsel urged strongly that they might, on the evidence, find the prisoners guilty of the minor offence of manslaughter.

After Maule had summed up the case and underlined the distinction between murder and manslaughter, the jury found Aaron Hagley guilty of the lesser charge and acquitted the other two prisoners. Hagley was sentenced to be transported for life, while his brother and Maslen, both charged with being in an enclosed ground in the night, armed with intent to kill game, were sentenced to six months' imprisonment and hard labour.

# 12

# DEATH OF A TAX COLLECTOR

## *Clayhidon, 1853*

As Jonathan May had found out to his cost, it was unwise for a wealthy man to flaunt his earthly riches too openly, or even to carry them around in public. Less than twenty years after May's murder, William Blackmore would also pay for doing so – with his life.

In 1853 Mr Blackmore, a miller, land surveyor and tax collector, aged fifty-three, lived with his wife Joan and their son, also named William, at the Mill in Clayhidon, a village in the Blackdown Hills, close to the Somerset border. On the morning of Saturday 5 February 1853 Blackmore left his house to collect tithes (agricultural taxes) from the local farmers. One of his first calls that day was at Burcombe Farm, the property of John Honeyball, where he collected about £5. Next he called at Mr Burford's farm for a similar sum, and

*Clayhidon Mill, home of the Blackmore family.* (Courtesy of Clayhidon Local History Group)

from the rest of the houses on his round he obtained about £20 altogether. While on the road, at about 5 p.m., he met Honeyball and three of his labourers – George Sparks, his brother Edmund and James Hitchcock, all of whom were in their twenties. George had recently become engaged to Hitchcock's daughter. Blackmore told Honeyball that he had been to his house and collected his tithes, presumably from his wife or one of the servants.

After a brief conversation, Blackmore left them. As he walked away, George Sparks was heard to comment under his breath, 'I think that man gathers more money than anyone else in the parish.' The labourers then went to Honeyball's house to collect their wages, and each one was offered a drink.

At about 6 p.m. Hitchcock and George Sparks left for the White Horse Inn at the corner of Gatchells Lane. Blackmore had just finished his work for the day and joined them about two hours later. He had already been offered a mug of cider or ale at most of the houses he had visited and was rather tipsy by now. So, possibly, were the two men he had seen earlier on. Edmund Sparks arrived at the inn a little later in the evening. To Ann Redwood, the landlady, Blackmore mentioned that he had a pain in his stomach, which he attributed to having drunk some of Farmer Warren's ale earlier on. Evidently the hair of the dog was the best solution, as he took a seat by the fire and downed three pints of Mrs Redwood's beer. Later he had a game of cards with George Sparks, and as they played they drank several quarts of ale mixed with brandy and sugar. Sparks could not afford to pay his share of the rounds and played cards for drink, but he was evidently a poor player and ended up owing Blackmore three pints. At one stage of the evening, it was noticed that George Sparks and James Hitchcock left the others and returned after a few minutes.

Blackmore paid for the drink with a half-crown, saying that was all the money he had in the world. Though he had been drinking on and off throughout much of the day, he was sober enough to take care not to reveal to them how much money he was actually carrying at the time. It would have been better for him if he had had the forethought to leave most of the tithes at home before visiting his regular watering hole. Subsequent events would prove that he had indeed overlooked such an obvious precaution.

Hitchcock grinned at him. 'You needn't be afeard of us, master – I won't rob 'e,' George Sparks assured him, 'Master isn't afeard of us, I know.' 'No! be gums,' Blackmore added. At about 1.20 a.m. all four men left together. Blackmore was not too enthusiastic about the other three's insistence on accompanying him home. Perhaps he was beginning to regret having socialised so much with them during the evening and suspected them of planning something. On their walk home they met another labourer, James Marks, who was the last person to see them all together.

Edmund Sparks went straight to his house, about half a mile from Blackmore's own home. Significantly, the conditions that night would later help those involved in tracking the footprints of Blackmore and his associates. Recent heavy rain had obliterated any old prints, and late at night and early next morning a sharp frost showed new ones very clearly. They were easy enough to trace when daylight came.

Blackmore parted company with the other two at French Nut Tree, and continued on his own towards Clayhidon Mill. He was unaware that they were following him, and that Sparks was carrying a pair of tongs which he had probably just taken from the blacksmith's shop opposite the inn.

When Blackmore did not return by 4 a.m., his wife and son William started to become anxious. William and James Howe, a miller who lived in the same road, went out with a candle and a lantern to search for him. Within a few minutes they discovered his body only a few yards from the house. He lay across the road, his skull and jaw fractured, but still warm and clearly not long dead. They found that the watch in his pocket had stopped at 1.43 a.m.; it was partly crushed, as if it had been struck by a heavy blow. A purse was by his side containing plenty of cash, but two £5 notes were later found to be missing.

Later that morning, Constable George Braddick apprehended the suspects. George Sparks was lodging with Edmund, and when Braddick arrived, George was still in bed. At first he denied any knowledge of the crime. He was then asked to get dressed in the clothes he had been wearing the night before, and when he did so, several spots of blood were visible on his waistcoat. His boots were examined and found to have a rather distinctive pattern of nails and tips. Their shape and size were checked against the footprints in the frost on the road and they corresponded exactly. The prints of Blackmore's boots were checked as well and from the patterns of each it was deduced that Sparks had run across a field in order to get in front of Blackmore. Some of the marks revealed traces of blood.

The house and outhouse buildings were thoroughly searched from top to bottom, and eight sovereigns and five half-sovereigns were found wrapped up in a piece of rag. This tallied with the amount Blackmore was believed to have had in his purse after he finished his work. Braddick showed George the money and George confessed, admitting there was nothing for him to gain from telling any lies. He then picked up a pair of tongs and struck with them as if inflicting a heavy blow, admitting that he had taken a similar pair from a neighbour's house and struck Blackmore. He knocked him down on the road and had only intended to rob him, but thought he had killed him with the first blow. Hitchcock, he said, was innocent. The tongs were later found in a stream not far from where Blackmore had been killed.

An inquest was held on Tuesday 8 February at the Half Moon Inn, Clayhidon, before Mr R.H. Aberdoin, the district coroner. George Sparks exonerated the others from the murder. Apart from the fact that Sparks had been in his company, there was no evidence against Edmund, and the only suspicious circumstances regarding Hitchcock were the spots on his greatcoat, which might or might not have been blood, and the footmarks in the frost on the road near where the body was found. Nevertheless, both George Sparks and Hitchcock were committed for trial at the ensuing county assizes.

The case came to Crown Court at Exeter on 18 March, with Mr Collier and Mr Karslake as counsel for the prosecution, John Coleridge and Mr Bere for the defence of Sparks, and Mr Ring for Hitchcock. Sparks admitted that he had struck Blackmore and killed him, though his intention was merely to commit robbery. Hitchcock said he had left both men and gone home to bed. He had not seen Sparks holding any iron objects, though in the small hours of a dark February morning it was unlikely that he would have seen anything much. A surgeon confirmed that there had been several blows to the victim's head, which had caused death. They had been inflicted by a heavy instrument, most probably the tongs. When young William Blackmore came to give evidence in court he produced his father's canvas purse and pressed his hands firmly against the underside of the dock desk, casting what was described as 'a feverish glance' at those around him. To the horror of nearly everybody present, the purse was covered in blood.

Mr Ring called on the jury to acquit Hitchcock as he was obviously innocent. Mr Coleridge then addressed the jury for Sparks. The evidence was so overwhelming that he could hardly ask them to acquit him. It had been said by an eminent judge, Mr Coleridge reported, that the advocate who would stand up and urge for an acquittal when the evidence was perfectly clear endeavoured to make the jury scoundrels and was thus no less a scoundrel himself. While he would not ask them to return a verdict of not guilty, he would submit to them that there were mitigating circumstances in that both parties were 'excited by liquor' and that there had been a quarrel between them. On the way home, Sparks had struck Blackmore and killed him, but the crime was therefore manslaughter and not murder.

In summing up, Mr Justice Crompton said that if the jury were satisfied that both prisoners committed the murder, or if the deed was done by one with the other standing by as an accessory, they were bound to find both men guilty. If they could take Mr Coleridge's view, they would reduce the offence to manslaughter, but they must not do so unless they could find some evidence to lead them to such a conclusion. The jury retired for just under half an hour.

While the trial was in progress, George Sparks showed no signs of being afraid of the outcome. He was confident that the defence's plea of manslaughter would ensure a spell of imprisonment but no more. But when the jury returned, he looked as though he was barely able to support himself. He must have foreseen his fate. Sparks was found guilty of murder and the man whom he had expected to become his father-in-law was not guilty. Too much alcohol might explain Sparks's actions but it could hardly excuse him from punishment.

# Trial Confession & Death !

On Friday morning Mr. Justice Crompton took his seat at nine o'clock. An immense number of people gathered round every approach to the court. At half past nine o'clock the prisoners, George Sparkes, 26, and James Hitchcock, 40, were placed at the bar, and arraigned for the wilful murder of Mr. Wm. Blackmore.

The prisoners who are labourers of the lowest class, were both shabbily dressed. The younger one was fresh coloured, and ruddy, with light hair. The elder ashy pale, with dark hair, and high retreating head. The younger, the actual murderer, had nothing ferocious in his aspect, while the son of the deceased got up to give evidence, and produced the purse of his murdered father, from which the gold and silver had been taken he pressed his hands firmly against the under side of the dock desk, and cast averted and feverish glances at the witness—who brought the evidence of blood guiltiness against him—for the purse, a large canvass bag, was all covered with gore.

The counsel for the prosecution were, Mr. Collier and Mr. Karslake; for the defence, Mr. Coleridge, Mr. Ring and Mr. Bere.

The prisoners having answered to their names and the jury being sworn.

The CLERK of ARRAIGNS said—George Sparkes and James Hitchcock, you are indicted for the wilful murder of William Blackmore, at Clayhidon, on the 6th of Feby.

George Sparkes are you guilty or not guilty?
Sparkes—Not guilty.
CLERK of ARRAIGNS—James Hitchcock—Are you guilty or not guilty?
Hitchcock—Not guilty.

in the morning. About three or four in the afternoon Mr. Honeyball was coming back with the two prisoners, and at this place they met Mr. Blackmore. Mr. Blackmore and Mr Honeyball exchanged civilities and the latter said " I've been at your house and got some money—I am going on to Farmer Warren's to get some more." That was said in the presence of Sparkes and Hitchcock. He then passed on—Sparkes observing at the time "Mr. Blackmore collects a quantity of money—more than anybody else in the neighbourhood." When Mr. Blackmore, therefore, was on his journey, these men were aware that he had money in his possession, and that he was going to collect more. Mr. Blackmore next called upon Mr. Rendle but did not get anything. He then called upon Mr. T. Warren and Mr. W. Warren, from whom he received £5 each. Altogether he had four sums of about £5 each. Here was the end of Mr. Blackmore's circuit that day. He then had to come back towards his home. Sparkes and Hitchcock, after passing Mr. Blackmore went to Mr. Honeyball's house, where they had something to drink and received trifling sums of money ; Hitchcock was paid 2s 4d and Sparkes was lent 3s. They left Honeyball's about six & went towards the White Horse Inn, which is 5 or 6 minutes walk, but did not arrive at the inn until 7 or 8 o'clock. Having had some drink, Sparkes went to the outer door and staid there. Between eight and nine Mr Blackmore came ; Sparkes was outside the door and spoke to him. Mr Blackmore, unfortunately for himself, remained drinking with the prisoners until past one in the morning. The landlady would depose that Sparkes made a signal to Hitchcock whilst there and both left for a short time. Edmund Sparkes, a brother of George, was there also, at 20 minutes past one all left. Edmund Sparkes and the deceased going first, the prisoners following. Edmund Sparkes left on arriving at his cottage, the prisoners and deceased went on. Both prisoners admit that they went with deceased as far as the French nut tree ; just beyond which was Edmund Sparkes cottage, and a little

Mr. COLERIDGE then addressed the Jury in defence of Sparkes He said he felt an overwhelming responsibility rested upon him that he stood between the prisoner and the Jury, and asked them to return a verdict, such as would be in accordance with the law, of their country, but to have a due regard for the life which they were about to decide the fate of. A man's life,—and perhaps a man's immortal soul—was in peril to-day, and it demanded the greatest consideration at their hands. He would tell them what he did not intend to ask at their hands. He did not intend for a single moment to ask of them, what it would be perfectly idle, from the evidence brought before them, to ask them to believe he was not guilty. A very distinguished ornament of the judicial bench was reported to have said on one occasion, that the man who attempted to persuade a jury in such a case to give a verdict of not guilty, was attempting to persuade them to become a set of scoundrels, and was no better than a scoundrel himself. He did not ask them to do so, and he trusted not one gentleman of the profession of which he was the humblest member, should so degrade himself, or the profession to which he belonged, by so acting. But he would briefly and simply tell them what he contended before them—and he trusted he should satisfy them that they would be justified—and if justified, they would be bound to say, that George Sparkes was guilty merely of the crime of manslaughter. He asked them to find by their verdict that he did kill Mr. Blackmore, but that he did not murder him. During the delivery of the eloquent speech, which was of some length, many of the auditors were deeply affected.

His LORDSHIP after summed up, and the jury retired, after an absence of a quarter of an hour they returned and gave a verdict of Guilty against George Sparkes and of Not Guilty against James Hitchcock.

His LORDSHIP said that, after a most attentive and patient trial, the prisoner Sparkes had been found guilty of a most barbarous murder. He

*Detail from a broadsheet announcing the 'trial confession and death' in the Blackmore murder case.*
*(Courtesy of Clayhidon Local History Group)*

Mr Justice Crompton might have wished for a different verdict. Several women were in the public gallery and most, if not all, were in tears. Though he might quite reasonably have been expected not to let his emotions show, the judge was deeply affected and he also wept; his sobs could be heard throughout the court and for a while he was unable to proceed. At length he delivered the sentence of death, 'in so low a tone as scarcely to be audible to the reporters'.

On being taken to the prison, Sparks became hysterical. However, he soon resigned himself to his fate and seemed to find some solace in the ministrations of the Chaplain, the Revd Mr Hollings, and the Governor, Mr Rose. Several applications were made to the High Sheriff, Mr E.B.H. Gennye, to fix an earlier time for the execution, as was generally the practice in London where hangings were carried out at around 8 a.m. He declined to comply, insisting that the execution would take place at midday as usual.

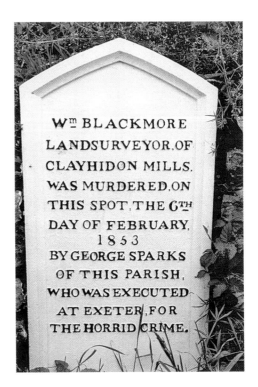

*The memorial stone at the bottom of Battle Street, close to the site where William Blackmore was killed.* (Courtesy of Clayhidon Local History Group)

On 1 April a crowd of over 10,000, mostly women, gathered at the gaol to watch as 'the unfortunate man was launched into eternity'. A reporter for the *Exeter Flying Post* was dismayed at the preponderance of women and remarked on 'the broadcloth of the middle classes jostling the cotton of the mechanics and labourers – a strange motley for so sad a scene and too painfully indicative of the fact, that the "lower orders" are not the only people who relish the sight of a public strangulation'. Five churches were opened for the purpose of 'providing sinners with a passport to the skies', but very few of those who had gone along to see the spectacle availed themselves of such repentance.

A memorial stone was later erected close to the mill at the bottom of Battle Street where the crime took place.

# 13

# THE GLOVE-MAKER AND THE CHIMNEY-SWEEP

## *Langtree, 1854*

As the crime historian Colin Wilson observed in *Murder in the Westcountry*, because nearly everybody knows everybody else in such close-knit communities, rural crimes tend to be solved more quickly. But there are always exceptions to this rule, like the case of Archibald Reed, the riverkeeper (see p. 94). However, the police in Victorian Devon often found it helpful that some areas within their jurisdiction were so remote that there was always somebody who knew other people's business and movements, especially if they were suspicious. If any strangers were in the area, a description could normally be supplied, and if a crime was committed, the miscreant would probably find no hiding place. This was what happened in 1854 when Mary Richards was raped and murdered in a relatively remote part of North Devon – the guilty man was remanded in custody within hours.

Mary Richards was a quiet, God-fearing girl of about twenty-one. She lived with her mother, Betty, at Langtree and helped to support her by making gloves for Agnes Wills, a shopkeeper at Torrington, 5 miles away. At around midday on 16 May 1854 Mary left her home for the shop, carrying the few pairs of gloves she had just finished. She also took with her two baskets, two dresses, a collecting card for the chapel and a shopping list including sugar, currants and saffron, to buy for a neighbour, Mary Ann Tucker. Arriving at Torrington, she did her errands, collected some belongings she had left at a friend's cottage, and at about 4 p.m. she set out for home with the shopping, walking up the long, steep Croft Hill.

She never reached her destination. At about 5 a.m. next day a shoemaker, William Milford, was walking past a row of fir trees at the top of the hill and heard groaning coming from a field adjoining the road. Going to investigate, he found Mary, her face and clothes covered with blood, lying in a ditch. Her dress was torn and one shoe was missing.

At that point another man, William Ward, drove by in a cart. Milford stopped him and between them they lifted her up carefully. As they moved

Mary, the crown of her bonnet fell from her head and they were horrified to see the brain oozing from a large wound in the skull. They asked her who she was and though very weak she was able to tell them she was the daughter of Betty Richards. She was trembling and suddenly became violently sick.

Meanwhile, Betty had been sitting up all night, waiting for her daughter's return. At about the same time as the men found Mary she left the house to look for the girl, reaching the field shortly after Milford and Ward. Horrified by their discovery, she spoke to Mary, who asked her in a weak voice if she could have some warm tea. Having probably been lying in the ditch for at least twelve hours overnight and in a state of extreme shock, she was very cold. Other people arrived and one went to fetch a surgeon, Dr John Oliver Rouse. After he had examined her, she was gently lifted into the cart and taken to the union workhouse. So far she had been unable to say what had happened to her, or by whom she had been injured.

On further examination Dr Rouse found Mary's hair was clotted with blood, and when he cut a large amount out, he saw thirteen wounds on her head. The bone was broken on the temple, there was an extensive scar 1 inch in diameter and a heavy bruise on the right side of the head. Her skull was smashed, and after he removed a piece of straw bonnet from her wound, he discovered that the membranes that covered her brain were broken. A blow must have been inflicted with a heavy blunt instrument. Further examination revealed that she had also been raped.

When she came round, the doctor told her that her condition was hopeless and that she would not recover from her injuries. (One might think that in a similar case today, he would be a little less honest and try to give her some hope of survival, even if he knew she had no chance.) Though she was barely able to speak, somehow she found the strength to tell her mother the names of the people she wanted to bear her to her grave and the hymns she would like for her funeral. She then recited the verse of a hymn which she wanted engraved on her headstone.

Suspicion fell immediately on a chimney-sweep, Llewellyn Garret Talmage Harvey, a distinctive-looking man with long sandy whiskers who had been in the vicinity of Torrington on the afternoon of 16 May. He had been born in the Oxford area, the illegitimate child of a tradesman, and received a good education. As a young adult he had visited the United States of America and claimed that while he was there he had taken part in activities with the Bible Christians, but later admitted this to be untrue. He was married, though there was no record of any children. He had a history of petty theft and his living as a chimney-sweep gave him ample opportunity to identify suitable properties for future burglaries. Shortly after moving to Devon he had been imprisoned for sheep stealing. One account says that he was transported to Australia for the offence, but had this been carried into effect he would not have returned so quickly, if at all. It is more likely that he was threatened with such a sentence, which was then commuted to imprisonment. He had been seen speaking to Mary when she entered the cottage on the road home to collect her things and again in Torrington later that same day.

Abraham Oldham, police superintendent at Barnstaple, was put in charge of the case, and on 17 May he went round various lodging and public houses in the town to check on any strangers who might have arrived within the previous twenty-four hours. At 1 a.m. he went to investigate a brothel where he found Harvey standing naked by the bed with a handkerchief round his head. Oldham asked him who he was, to be told brusquely, 'That's my business and not yours.' 'I must know something about you,' Oldham insisted. 'If you must know, I came last from South Molton', was the answer. Noticing that the man looked as if he had recently sported whiskers but was freshly shaved, Oldham asked him where he had visited a barber, to be told 'at Porlock'. Then he arrested him on suspicion of 'an aggravated outrage'. Harvey denied knowing anything about the attack on Mary Richards, but he was made to get dressed, taken downstairs and handed over to one of the policemen who had accompanied Oldham. He tried to escape, but after a scuffle he was recaptured.

The same day he was taken before the magistrate. At first he refused to give his name or say anything about himself. After considering his position, he gave in and supplied his name and address. Oldham then took him to see Mary Richards, where she lay helpless in her bed at the workhouse, and she confirmed that he was the last man she had seen. She fixed her eyes on him while he stood there and, not surprisingly, she seemed afraid of him. He was present at Rouse's examination. Another constable, James Terrell, went to search Harvey's home on 18 May, and found a hammer with bloodstains on it and a few blades of fresh grass between the claws.

During the next few days Mary drifted in and out of consciousness. At times she was quite lucid and made an effort to carry on normal conversation. George Henry Sellick, master of the union, saw her on 19 May. She said she had sent for him so he could take down in writing what she could remember about Harvey. She proceeded to give a detailed account of his attack on her. At one time Rouse thought she might make a reasonable recovery, or at least live for about another year, but it was not to be. In a few days she took a turn for the worse, and her mother stayed by her bedside for most of the time as she lingered, her periods of unconsciousness becoming longer, until she died on 30 May. A post-mortem found that the rest of her body was perfectly healthy and death was caused by injuries to the brain.

The case came to trial at Exeter Summer Assizes on 24 July. The first witnesses to be called by the prosecution were Milford and Ward. Among those who followed were surgeon Rouse, Sellick and Betty Richards. A blacksmith from Little Torrington, George Gribble, said he had been on the town bridge on the day of the attack and saw the prisoner; at first he thought he was fishing, but then he noticed he appeared to be doing nothing. He saw something projecting from his right-hand trouser pocket, which he thought must have been a stick, until he looked more carefully and noticed it was a knife.

Mary Allen, another glove-maker, lived at Sutcombe, 12 miles from Torrington. She said she had come into the town that day with some gloves, and that she knew Harvey fairly well. When she saw him sitting on a bank by the roadside they exchanged a few words, and he asked her how long it would be before she returned. She said it would not be for a while. At first he started to follow her, then said he would wait for her. He looked at what she was carrying, said it was a fine basket of work and added she was bound to get paid well for it. She found something disquieting about his manner, then saw what she assumed to be a knife in his pocket – only now did she realise it must have been the hammer. Nervously she humoured him before hurrying away.

Agnes Wills confirmed that Mary Richards had brought her some gloves on 16 May between 10 a.m. and 2 p.m. She paid her 4s 7½d, and gave her some leather to make up a few more pairs. On the next day she saw the prisoner at her shop, bringing in some gloves made by his sister-in-law, Agnes Dale. As she paid him, she asked if he had heard about the sad news in the area and he told her he had not. Policemen had been at her house just before he called at the shop and she mentioned that constables were out in full force, looking for a man whom she described as having the appearance of an Irish vagrant with sandy whiskers. With this he said 'Good morning' and left the shop. He told her he was a chimney-sweep and she observed that his linen seemed unusually clean for somebody in that particular trade.

Grace Short, a widow who lived at Taddiport, said that on 16 May she saw a young woman walk past her shop carrying two baskets. She also noticed a man following her up the hill and was sure the prisoner was that same man. Another resident of Taddiport, Mary Haywood, recalled having seen Mary at about 3.30 that afternoon. A man in a black long-tailed coat and black high-crowned hat was following her. She heard him say to her, 'You have got to journey's end', to which she assured him that she had several miles to go. She then turned into the house of Haywood's next-door neighbour, Mary Martin.

Several other witnesses came forward to confirm that they had seen Harvey in the area that day. Among them was Thomas Stacey, who had been walking past the fir trees at the scene of the attack. Rather oddly, he noticed what he described as fresh blood, but heard no crying, nor anything else suspicious, and he saw no reason to make a search of the area.

Abraham Lamb, a barber at Barnstaple, recalled the prisoner coming to him in the afternoon and asking to be shaved. As Lamb was putting the lather on the prisoner's face, Harvey asked for his whiskers to be shaved off, high under the hair on his head. While the barber did so, he asked him about the distances to Wiveliscombe and Ilfracombe. On the following day Lamb identified him at the station house as the man he had shaved. After this the prisoner's statement was read out to the court. It was a long, rambling account, which said nothing about meeting the deceased, and only asserted his innocence.

At 6.30 p.m. the trial was adjourned. Throughout the proceedings Harvey was seen continually making notes in pencil to send to his counsel. They were written at high speed, which impressed the spectators in court. The sitting was resumed by Mr Justice Wightman at 9 a.m. on 25 July. Mr John Coleridge addressed the jury on the prisoner's behalf, but his task was a hard one. All he could do was express general observations on the brutality of the crime and the disgust that every man must feel. Though there can scarcely have been a man in court who had not made up his mind on a conviction, he continued, he asked the jury 'to dismiss from their minds anything they had heard or read on the subject'. Mr Justice Wightman summed up the case, but it only took the jury a few minutes to arrive at their verdict of guilty.

In prison awaiting execution, Harvey confessed that he was guilty of the murder and acknowledged that the sentence was a just and righteous one. He stated that he had left his house with the hammer in his pocket and had gone out determined to kill a woman or young girl at random. Mary Allen had had a fortunate escape because he had initially resolved to make her his victim, but somehow he lost his nerve. It was the tragedy of Mary Richards to cross his path by chance later that day and to pay the ultimate penalty of fate.

After he had been convicted, he sought the attendance of several local ministers of the Wesleyan Methodists, to which body he represented himself as belonging. Accordingly three of them attended him constantly until the day of his trial, after which they handed him over into the spiritual care of the chaplain of the gaol. He behaved himself well and hoped that he might still be acquitted. Once it was made clear that there would be no reprieve from his sentence, he resigned himself to his fate and asked the ministers to apologise to Mr Justice Wightman for 'the bold conduct which he displayed during his trial'. He likewise expressed his indebtedness for the powerful and eloquent speech made on his behalf by Mr Coleridge for the defence, and then had a last farewell meeting with his wife.

Harvey had been serving a custodial sentence for stealing sheep at Exeter gaol at the very time that George Sparks had been executed sixteen months earlier. Coincidentally, on Friday 4 August 1854, he was the next person to go to the gallows at the same premises.

# 14

# THE TORQUAY BABY FARMER

## Torquay, 1865

In the nineteenth century there was considerable social stigma attached to mothers who bore children out of wedlock. Before the advent of adoption agencies and social services, untrained women would offer fostering facilities at a price to mothers desperate to be relieved of their illegitimate offspring. Some of these babies were sold to childless couples who were keen to adopt them. Others were killed, simply because they proved difficult to place or because the 'baby farmers' were unscrupulous enough to make money by pocketing the cash desperate (and often almost penniless) mothers gave them, and then disposing of infants by murder when it proved difficult to make a quick profit by rehoming them with well-to-do couples. The baby farmers relied on the probability that even if the mother suspected anything, she would be too frightened or ashamed to inform the police. It was easy for such women to get rid of children with little, if any, fear of detection. Abortion was against the law, and backstreet terminations carried a high risk of the pregnant woman suffering a fatal haemorrhage. It was also illegal for women to abandon their children, and killing their infants usually resulted in the death penalty, until the Infanticide Act of 1922 forbade execution on such grounds. Almost every area of Victorian Britain had its own sorry cases of baby farming which ended in murder, and Devon was no exception.

On 16 October 1864 Mary Jane Harris, aged twenty-three, was employed as a servant by Mrs Gibson of Upper Union Lane, Torquay. She gave birth to a boy at the house, and gave him the names Thomas Edwin Gibson Harris, though he was never baptised. She was unmarried, and this was her second child; both, she later admitted, were by the same father. She and her baby remained at the premises until she was able to obtain a similar post with another lady in Torquay, a Mrs Wansey. Mrs Gibson, one must assume, has to have been more kindhearted or broadminded than most other women of the day in a similar position. Most employers would probably not have thought twice about throwing Miss Harris and her child out on to the streets at a moment's notice, but Mrs Gibson was prepared to let the infant and his mother stay on at her house for a few more weeks.

During this time Miss Harris's sister and mother, and Thomas's father, Mr Nicholls, took it in turns to pay her visits. The latter was described by the press as 'a well-to-do farmer', but it seems he was not prepared to assume any responsibility for mother and child, not offering them a home or even allowing the baby to bear his name. On 19 November Mr Prowse, the registrar, came to the house and registered the birth.

Perhaps Mrs Wansey was less generous than Mrs Gibson, for within two months Miss Harris had decided that she would have to do what most other mothers in her circumstances invariably did and get rid of her unwanted infant, or at least find someone to take him off her hands for a while. On 12 December she handed him over to Charlotte Winsor, a grandmother aged forty-five, who promised she would take charge of little Thomas for a fee of 3s per week. Mrs Winsor and her husband were farmers; Charlotte Pratt, their seven-year-old granddaughter, lived with them, and enjoyed helping to nurse Thomas.

On 5 February 1865 Miss Harris called on Mrs Gibson, and told her she was going to take Thomas and leave him in the care of her aunt who lived on Dartmoor. A few days later Miss Harris was seen at Mrs Winsor's cottage, nursing baby Thomas on her lap. Mrs Winsor asked Charlotte to run a shopping errand for her, and the little girl was away for about an hour. When she came back she found both her grandmother and Miss Harris there, but Thomas was gone. Charlotte had become very attached to him and asked where he was, only to be told by Miss Harris that her aunt had just fetched him. In order to distract Charlotte's attention, Mrs Winsor gave her 2d and asked her to go and buy some buns. On her return, Mary Harris told Charlotte that she had been taken to the station to meet her aunt, and the baby had been taken away to the other side of Exeter.

On 16 February Charlotte saw Mrs Winsor washing Thomas's clothes, and noticed her putting them into a carpet bag. Mrs Winsor then picked the bag up and took Charlotte for a walk towards the Torre Abbey turnpike gate. After they had gone a little way down the road they went to Mary Harris's house. Mrs Winsor left her granddaughter by the Castle Inn, close to Harris's home, continued for a while, and later returned with the empty bag.

On the previous day, a group of people walking in the direction of the Winsors' house had noticed a parcel lying beside the road. When they examined it they found a wrapper sewn up with string, and inside was the naked body of a baby boy about four months old, wrapped in a copy of the *Western Times* dated 6 May 1864. They took the body to the police, who searched the registry of births, and decided it was probably the infant registered by Mary Ann Harris. A police officer traced her to Mrs Wansey's house. Under questioning, she admitted having given birth to a child in the previous October. When asked where the baby was she said he had been at Mrs Winsor's house, but her aunt had taken him away. She said she had heard that a dead child had been picked up, but hoped they would not think it was hers. The police thought she seemed genuinely distressed and close to fainting.

On 19 February Mrs Gibson had met Mary Harris and talked about a child that had just been found on the moor. This may have been a coincidence – Torquay was some distance from the nearest part of Dartmoor – but 'the moor' might also have referred to any rural area of land in South Devon. Mrs Gibson told her that she had dreamed it was her child, that Mrs Winsor had killed it, and that Miss Harris was going to be hanged for the crime. Mary Harris begged her not to say such a thing, and then told her she had to go and see the dressmaker about a bonnet. She went and returned in a minute, asking Mrs Gibson to go up the lane with her because she thought she could hear a child crying by the wall. Mrs Gibson accompanied her, and told her that all she could hear was a cat mewing.

The police obtained a warrant, went to the house and read it to Miss Harris. 'Go to Mrs Winsor's and she'll tell you where my child is', was her reaction. She was taken into custody. On the way to the station, she asked, 'Do you think if I can't give an account of my child that I shall be hung?' The police did not answer.

Next day the police went to Mrs Winsor's house. They asked how long it had been since the child was taken away and were told that Thomas had now been gone for a month. Though she had never learned to write, Mrs Winsor showed them an almanac and pointed out that she had made a mark against the date of 12 December 1864 when she received the baby, but had not made any mark when he was taken away. Asked to describe the 'aunt' who had fetched him, she said she had been 'a tallish woman, red face, dark complexion', about forty years of age, wearing a dark bonnet, a coloured shawl and an alpaca gown. The child, she said, was plump, with a long thin nose, of light complexion, with light to dark hair, and a wart on its toe. She added that she hoped 'nothing had happened to it, pretty dear'. They asked when she had last seen the mother. She replied that it was on the previous Sunday night between 8 and 9 p.m., and that she and the father had accompanied Miss Harris part of the way home as she felt afraid to be out on her own.

The police told her they would need to make a thorough search of the premises where she was living and she made no objection. When they looked they found a child's hood, which she said belonged to her own baby. When asked where it was, she pointed to a box, which contained only a doll. When they commented what a strange baby it was, she said it belonged to her daughter's child at Plymouth.

Though she protested that she knew 'nothing about it', she was still remanded in custody and escorted to Torquay town hall, where Miss Harris was also detained. When Harris saw Mrs Winsor she burst into tears and asked to speak to the sergeant, who led her into an adjoining room. If Mrs Winsor had done anything to the baby, she asked between sobs, what would be her punishment, and would she herself be punished too? He did not answer. She then asked him if he had seen what Winsor did; he shook his head. She said Winsor had put her finger across her neck, which she took as a sign that she (Harris) would be hanged. Did he think she would? Once again, the policeman said nothing.

Questioning was resumed the following day. Miss Harris was in the office and said that Mrs Winsor told her to say the child was at her aunt's house. 'Why won't you let me see the child?' Miss Harris asked, distraught. 'If you'll let me see it I will tell you in a minute whether it is mine or not; my child has no mark on it whatever.'

Soon she realised there was nothing to be gained by feigning ignorance. 'I had better tell the truth and no lies about it,' she said. The policeman warned her to be careful what she said, as it would be used against her. 'If you'll go and fetch Winsor,' she went on, 'I'll tell you all about it; I've told part, but not the whole. It is not my child that's been picked up, but if you'll go and fetch Winsor I'll tell you all about it. If you'll show me the child I'll tell you in a moment.'

When Mrs Winsor came voluntarily to the police station a little later, she called out 'Hello, Mary' to Harris, who ignored her. After being taken into another room for questioning, Mrs Winsor said she had been told Miss Harris was there for murdering her child, but she did not believe it. 'Her aunt took the child away from me a month ago last Tuesday. I've got a private mark on the child; I should know it, among ten thousand; it has a wart on its right foot, close behind its great toenail. It's a fine little baby, and has a lot of hair on the top of its head. It was a month old when I had it. I kept it six weeks, and it has been gone from me a month ago last Tuesday.'

Winsor was taken to the cell where the child's body lay. She took its leg in her right hand, looked at its great toe, and said that this was not 'her' child, as there was no wart to be seen and the leg was too large. When she asked to see the head, she denied again that it was Thomas Harris. 'I am very glad the child has gone from me, as I only had two shillings a week for keeping it, and I could not get any money before May's quarter was up.'

Mrs Edwards, who was responsible for searching the female prisoners, said that Miss Harris had twice told her she was sure she would be hanged: 'If I tell the truth shall I be hung?' Mrs Edwards told her that was nonsense: 'Who told you so?'

The prisoners, Miss Harris and Mrs Winsor, were sent for trial before Mr Baron Channell at the Exeter Spring Assizes on 17 March, and were jointly convicted of murder. Mr Carter and Mr Bere were counsel for the prosecution, Mr Prideaux and Mr Turner for Harris, and Mr Folkard for Winsor.

It became clear that there was no love lost between the two women, and each was equally intent on saving her own neck by blaming the other. An officer produced evidence of a conversation he had with Mrs Winsor when he visited her in her cell while the two were in custody. She asked him when he thought they would be put on trial, and told him 'that nasty Harris' would be transported.

> One night she came to my house to see the child, and was giving it something, which I thought was sugar candy. Afterwards the child made a noise, and dribbled, and I took the child and put my tongue to its little mouth to taste what she had been giving it. It was a sour taste, very acid. I said to Harris, 'You nasty Harris, what have you been giving it?' She said, 'Don't taste it, it will poison you.' I said, 'You nasty Harris, if it will poison me it will poison the child; what is it?' She said, 'It's what they give rats and mice, but we have been using it for cleaning brass and copper.' After that I got some warm water and milk for the child to drink, and she took something more from a paper and put into it. Then the child began to doze a little, and she went out to attend to her pigs.

When Mrs Winsor came back into the house, she said she saw Miss Harris was standing the child on its head in a saucepan full of water. 'For God's sake, what are you doing?' she asked in horror. 'Do you want to hang yourself and me too? You shall take the child away with you.' Harris then said her aunt was going to keep the child for 3s a week.

On the second day of proceedings, Charlotte Pratt was examined in court. Spending two hours in the witness box must have been a formidable ordeal for someone aged only seven, though the papers described her as 'very intelligent'. She related how Mary Harris had brought her baby to her grandmother's house, that her grandmother dressed and washed it, and she herself nursed it. At no stage did she notice any odd marks on the child's feet or anywhere else on the body. She mentioned the walk with her grandmother to Mrs Harris's house after Thomas's disappearance, and being shown his dead body – a rather macabre sight for such a young child, especially as this was a baby to whom she had become so attached. Significantly, she did not give the date when this occurred.

On cross-examination by Mr Folkard, she admitted her grandmother was very fond of the baby and never unkind to it, and Mary Harris used to come and see it regularly. She mentioned that a policeman had accompanied her to the spot where her grandmother had taken her, and had asked her if 'that was the place'. He had then given her 3d when she was at the town hall. She saw her grandmother put something in a cart when she went out with her for the first time, she said. When she was cross-examined by Mr Prideaux, Charlotte started to become confused, telling him, 'I never said I did not see anything put in the cart. My grandmother spoke to the man in the cart.' These statements were at some variance with her deposition to the court.

The testimony of Mrs Harris's aunt was produced. She had been unaware of the birth of the child until he was four months of age. She denied ever having fetched a child from Mrs Winsor's house, and when her niece was in custody she asked 'how she came to put the child upon her'. 'I did not know what to say,' was the prisoner's answer.

Dr Stabb, who was responsible for examining the body, told the court there was a mark on his face and nose as if it had been bitten by rats, which were known to be in Mrs Winsor's cellar. The baby had been well-nourished, all the organs were healthy, the stomach was two-thirds full of undigested biscuit food, and he could find nothing to account for its death. The lungs were congested, the body was very pale, some of the deep-seated vessels were full of blood and the superficial ones empty. The brain was slightly congested, and there was no trace of poison or disease. The most probable cause of death was exposure, and if the infant had been left outside in the prevailing weather conditions, an hour would have been enough to kill him. If chloroform had been used there would not have been any trace of it, and if the face had been immersed in water the appearance would have been the same. The food must have been given about half an hour before his death.

When cross-examined by Mr Folkard, Dr Stabb said that exposure in an open cart would have been enough to account for death if the child was not properly clothed. Initially he had thought that the symptoms were consistent with death within twelve hours of the examination. Had the body been kept in the house for a week, decomposition would have commenced. On cross-examination by Mr Prideaux, he said there was no appearance of decomposition. If the child had been buried in the snow it might have been preserved. It could have been held in water without any appearance of bruise or pressure. He saw no signs of any fit, and he did not think it died from natural causes. It was possible for a child to be drowned without there being any marks, he added. The symptoms, he believed, were consistent with immersion in water and then exposure, in which case the boy might have been dead for up to five days before he saw him. The judge remarked that there was nothing to show the baby did not die from suffocation. This closed the case for the prosecution.

Mr Folkard now addressed the jury on behalf of Mrs Winsor, saying that the evidence amounted to a case of suspicion and nothing more. On behalf of Miss Harris, Mr Prideaux dwelt on 'the single exception of the unhappy weakness which had induced her to yield to a not unnatural passion', and that in spite of this she 'stood before them as unblemished and as much entitled to their sympathy as it was possible for any young woman to be'. It was evident that she had been devoted to her child, and very reluctant to part with him. The doubts as to the child's identity and whether he had been murdered and, above all, the discrepancies in Miss Pratt's evidence, meant that the case could not be proved.

The jury were 'locked up' at 7 p.m. and remained sitting until midnight. When Mr Baron Channell was told that they could not reach agreement he discharged them, and the prisoners were ordered to be kept in custody.

A retrial was ordered, and they appeared at the Exeter Assizes again on 28 July before Mr Justice Keating. They were not called upon to plead again, and for the prosecution Mr Carter said he had been instructed to apply for leave to call Harris as a witness. For the defence, Mr Prideaux said he could make no objection, but asked if it would not be necessary that she should first be acquitted. The judge said he thought that unnecessary, and Harris was taken from the bar, so Winsor was on trial alone. She was called upon to challenge the jury but Mr Folkard, again defending her, objected on the grounds that the prisoner, 'having been once in peril' could not now be put on trial before another jury.

Several witnesses were called, though their information added very little to what was already known. One of the policemen stated that when the prisoner and Harris were in the magistrate's private room, Miss Harris asked Mrs Winsor if she had seen the child and the latter said she had. 'Was it mine?' Harris asked, only to be told after a pause, 'I can hardly tell after the child is dead,' adding after another pause, 'you will neither hang me nor transport me.'

Not surprisingly, Miss Harris's appearance in the witness box caused quite a sensation. After describing her confinement and the baby's birth, she told the court that on 10 December 1864 she had made an arrangement with the prisoner that Mrs Winsor would take care of him. She had previously asked two other people to do so but without success. While Thomas lived at the Winsors' house, she saw him four times, and on the last occasion she remarked that there had been a report of a baby having been 'picked up' nearby. The prisoner said, 'I wonder I had not got myself into it once before.' She had, she said, 'put away one for a girl who was confined at her house, who had promised to give her £2, but she did not give it her. I asked her how she did it. She said she put her finger under the jugular vein.' The prisoner, averred Harris, went on to describe cold-bloodedly having 'stifled one' at three weeks for another girl, throwing it into Torbay, 'and when it was picked up it was nearly all washed to pieces'. She had also 'put away one' for her own sister, Porey, on a promise of receiving £4 for the job, but she only received £2. As a result she had refused to speak to her sister ever since.

On Sunday 5 February Harris went to see the child at the prisoner's house, and when she got there about 7.30 a.m. she found the Winsors in bed. She knocked at the window, and when a voice asked who was there, she said she wanted to come in and see her child. Mr Winsor let her in, she went into the bedroom, and Mrs Winsor told her that she would not keep the child after March. She asked if Harris would like to come over one day during the week and fetch him, and the offer was accepted. Harris went on to describe going back later in the week, and how she was told that if she gave Mrs Winsor £5, the woman would do away with the child. She mentioned another visit on 9 February when the baby was tied to a chair and Charlotte Pratt was playing with him. After a while Mrs Winsor sent the little girl out and said, 'she did not do it [kill the baby] before I came out, because if I told on her I must tell on myself, for one would be as bad as the other'. Miss Harris said she would never tell if the crime were never discovered. Mrs Winsor asked her if she should kill the boy, and Mary asked how. Mrs Winsor said she would put the child between the bed ties, then took him into the bedroom, stayed ten minutes, came back without the baby, and asked Harris to look in, saying the baby would soon die. Later she came out with the baby, which was dead. She undressed it. They went into the bedroom and opened a box, Mrs Winsor wrapped the baby up in newspapers and put it into the box. After descriptions of further detail, Harris was cross-examined and said she had taken her trial for the offence. She swore that she did not attempt to poison the child herself; she wished him to live, but instead 'saw it barbarously murdered'.

The jury now had little doubt that Mrs Winsor was guilty of murder, and she was sentenced to be hanged in August. A few days before the sentence was to be carried out, it was ruled that there were doubts as to the legality of the discharge-without-a-verdict of the jury before whom the convict was tried for the same offence at the last Lent Assizes. Her counsel had found a loophole, and claimed that when a jury in a capital crime were discharged without giving a verdict, the proceedings were deemed irregular and therefore not legal. This was referred to the Lord Chancellor, who ruled that it ought to be submitted to the judges for their opinion, and sentence was deferred until 27 November 1865. *The Times* wrote that it was to be hoped that justice would 'not be defeated by such a technicality, and we rarely heard so strong a feeling evinced against any criminal'.

The execution was postponed until the question of law could be settled by a proper tribunal. A writ of error was brought and decided against the convict by the Court of the Queen's Bench, and the execution was scheduled for 11 February 1866. Crowds gathered to see Mrs Winsor suffer the full penalty of the law, and copies of a broadsheet were circulated, giving full details of her execution as if it had already taken place. In fact it turned out to be the hanging that never was, for at the last minute the Home Secretary granted a reprieve. William Calcraft, who was recognised at that time as the country's official executioner in all but name, had reached Exeter by the 3.30 p.m. train to carry out the sentence, and stayed in lodgings near the gaol overnight. On the following morning he was advised that on this occasion his services would not be required after all.

Though Charlotte Winsor had undoubtedly suffered from her prolonged period of imprisonment under sentence of death, she was lucky to escape the

THE GROANS
OF THE
GALLOWS,
Or the Past and Present
LIFE OF
WILLIAM CALCRAFT,

THE LIVING
*Hangman of Newgate.*

" The Cross shall displace the Gibbet,
and all will be accomplished."      Victor Hugo.

ENTERED AT STATIONERS' HALL.

*William Calcraft, who carried out the majority of executions in Britain between 1829 and his retirement in 1874. This portrait on the title page of his ghost-written memoirs,* The Groans of the Gallows, *first published in 1846, shows him at about the time of his appointment.*

gallows. When she appeared in court at Exeter for a third time in March 1866, the counsel for the defence read out a statement from the Secretary of State that all circumstances of the case had been taken into consideration, and as 'the prisoner had given her evidence in the most proper and satisfactory manner, no evidence should be offered for the prosecution'. Mr Justice Byles told the jury that they could not return a verdict of guilty as no evidence was offered against the prisoner, and on 11 May her death sentence was commuted to penal servitude for life. She remained in prison until her death thirty years later.

There is little doubt that she was guilty of a particularly callous and unpleasant murder, perhaps even several, if her chief witness was to be believed. Such had her notoriety become that within a few weeks, Madame Tussaud's, of Baker Street, London, was advertising in its new exhibition of waxworks at the Chamber of Horrors an effigy 'taken from life' of Charlotte Winsor.

# 15

# THE SHOEMAKER, HIS WIFE AND HER LOVER

## *Clyst Honiton, 1865*

In 1840 William and Mary Ann Ashford were married, both being around twenty-one years of age at the time. They lived in Clyst Honiton, a small, quiet village about 4 miles east of Exeter, where they had a shoemaker's business. According to the census returns of 1851, their address was 4 Victoria Cottages, though the Clyst Honiton burial records for 1865 give it as Duke of York Cottage. There appear to have been no children of the marriage.

William Ashford was a successful, thrifty and hard-working man of business, who had managed to save a considerable sum of money over the years. For much of the time he employed an apprentice. Census records for 1851 show that sixteen-year-old William Walrond was registered at the Ashfords' address in the capacity of 'cordwiner apprentice', as was bootmaker William Fish, aged thirty-two, although the latter is listed as merely a lodger. Walrond and Fish were reliable, hard-working young men who caused the Ashfords no problems. The same could not be said of a later live-in apprentice, William Pratt, who was appointed in about 1859.

After nearly twenty years of marriage Mary was becoming bored with her conscientious but perhaps rather dull husband, whom she sometimes felt paid more attention to his trade than to her. The arrival of good-looking, young William Pratt proved a temptation impossible for Mary to resist. As the newspapers were later to report, there could be 'no doubt that a criminal intimacy existed between them'. Aware that his wife and his employee were misbehaving behind his back, sometime around the end of 1863 William dismissed Pratt from his employment and ordered him to leave the house. Furious with his cheating spouse, William made a will in which he left all his property to his father and brother. Mary, meanwhile, continued a clandestine correspondence with Pratt, who had by now moved to Dawlish.

After eight months William Ashford reconsidered their position, and either realised that Pratt was too good a worker to lose, or was persuaded by his wife to let him return – perhaps a combination of both. By late 1864 Pratt was back at the cottage, and this time he was more circumspect in his behaviour. Having been given a second chance, he had seen the error of his ways, and 'his guilty passion seems to have cooled', no doubt much to the relief of his employer and presumably to the bitter disappointment of his employer's wife. Mary must have been even more mortified to learn that Pratt had recently become engaged to be married to a young woman in the village.

However, Mary and Pratt were both regularly seen together in public around Clyst Honiton, and their liaison was an open secret. She was still prepared to think she could win back his affections and get her hands on her husband's money. Already she had protested bitterly at being excluded from her husband's will, and this led to quarrels between them, as a result of which he reluctantly revoked the document. On 28 June 1865 he made another last will and testament which named her as the sole beneficiary.

On Wednesday 25 October 1865 Mary sent Selina Ann Ponsford, a young girl who lived nearby, to the chemist for some jalap, a drug which was then in common use as a laxative. The following Sunday, William Ashford had tea with a friend in the village, and in the course of conversation repeatedly expressed disgust with his wife's misconduct. Did he return home in a mood of bitterness and give her a piece of his mind? It was at this time that they were quarrelling, and not only in private. Angry scenes were seen and heard by others in the village. It may have been coincidence, but that evening Mary remarked with apparent concern to one of her neighbours, Police Constable Butt, that her husband had just become very ill with diarrhoea and general sickness. Next day he seemed a little better, but on the Tuesday he had deteriorated and she went to see Dr Lionel Roberts, a surgeon at Exeter. She described the symptoms to him, and he prescribed some medicine. That evening Emily Butt, the policeman's wife, called round to see how William was.

On the following morning Mary asked Dr Roberts to come and see her husband. He found the patient very weak and ill, constantly being sick, and complaining of great pain and thirst. He decided to change the medicine. On Thursday 2 November Roberts called again, and found the symptoms were just as bad as ever. That evening another neighbour, Mary Brewer, came to see them. While she was in the house Mary Ann mixed some medicine in the kitchen downstairs before bringing it up to William. Mary Brewer later said she thought there was nothing unusual in such an action.

On Friday William asked for a cup of tea, and his wife went downstairs to fetch him some. Mrs Butt had called again, and was sitting beside him in the bedroom. Mary brought the tea up, but then heard a knock at the door and went downstairs to answer it. While she did so Mrs Butt got up to pour out the tea, and on lifting the spoon she was surprised to notice signs of a bluish-white powder attached to it. She thought it was probably arrowroot and expected it would thicken the tea, so she gave William a cup. However, one sip was enough for him to decide he did not want any more. Afterwards, Mrs Brewer took some of the powder in her fingers, and was concerned to discover that it felt rather gritty.

Later that same day Dr Roberts saw William Ashford for a third time, and decided he would seek a second opinion. William asked for Dr Miles of Heavitree, whom he had seen before. Dr Miles arrived to find the patient in bed, his eyes protruding, his head bent backwards, his back arched and his limbs very stiff. He was just as puzzled by the case as his colleague, and could suggest no medicine other that that which had already been prescribed. Another visitor to the sickbed was William's younger brother, Thomas, who lived at St Thomas, Exeter. He had just received a letter from PC Butt warning him of the severity of William's condition. Mary took Thomas upstairs, and William greeted him sombrely with the words, 'Oh, I'm so very, very ill.' Thomas gave him some gin and peppermint, and stayed to talk to him for a while.

That night the patient had several seizures, and was in increasing agony throughout Saturday morning. He asked at least once for Dr Roberts, but either his wife delayed sending the message, or the doctor was too busy to come immediately. In view of the patient's serious condition, the latter is unlikely. It must be assumed that Mary did not want him to appear too promptly lest he should suspect what she was doing to the hapless patient. All the same, she invited Mrs Butt to come and stay at the house. During one of William's attacks Mrs Butt saw Mary sitting by the fire, saying nonchalantly, 'Stand back, let me look at him. Don't deceive me; one of those fits will carry him off.' On reflection it struck her as an unusually callous remark for a wife to make. She also noticed on the washstand a wine glass with a small deposit of powder settled at the bottom, similar to the substance she had found in William's tea. It looked rather suspicious, so when Mary was out of the room she scraped some out, putting it carefully in a piece of paper. Later she showed it to his brother, Thomas, and they guessed that it must be arsenic.

Mrs Butt stayed in the house to help, and during the afternoon she was in the kitchen cooking a meal for Mary when she heard what sounded like bumping going on upstairs. She went to the bedroom to check, and saw William out of bed having a fit, with Mary and another neighbour attending to him. Moments later Dr Roberts arrived. 'The man's dying,' he told them. 'What did you get him out of bed for?' 'He would get out,' they answered, as if unable to prevent him. At around 5 p.m. William's earthly sufferings were over.

Even after a post-mortem examination, two other doctors were unable to find any natural causes to account for the death. The deceased man's stomach, liver and samples of his vomit were placed in jars, sealed up and sent for further analysis to Mr Herapath at Bristol, after which he was given a funeral at St Michael's Church in the village. Mr Herapath discovered traces of arsenic and strychnine in the various samples, and gave his verdict that the symptoms were consistent with death occasioned by such poisons. The powder in the paper which Mrs Butt had discreetly taken from the wine glass was sent to him and also proved to be arsenic.

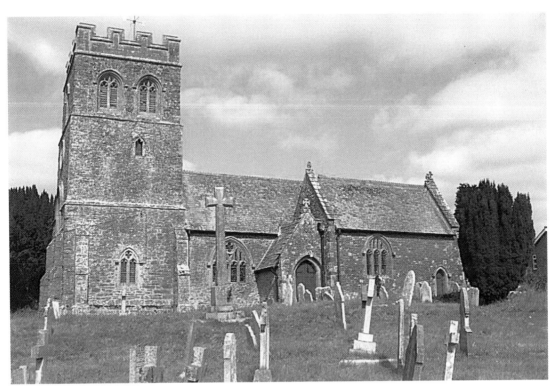

*St Michael's Church, Clyst Honiton.* (© Kim Van der Kiste)

Only one person had been in attendance on William Ashford when his illness began. PC Butt took Mary into custody that evening. When he asked her to come with him, she looked at him in horror and said, 'There is something, something; lock the door and tell me here.' He told her that he was not at liberty to explain any further while they were at her house, and she had to come to his place instead. When she agreed to accompany him, he charged her formally with causing her husband's death by administering poison. 'You cannot prove where I bought my arsenic,' she said. 'Oh, Mr Butt, I didn't do it.'

As he began to search her, she took from the pocket of her dress a prayer book, a purse, a pocket handkerchief and a small packet, which she threw into the fire. She had spilt part of the powder on her clothes, and wiped it off with the handkerchief. On examination this, too, turned out to be arsenic. White powder on the clasp of the purse was found to be strychnine mixed with starch. A further sample came to light on 10 November, six days after William's death, when Mrs Brewer was helping to clean the house. In the bedroom she found a screwed-up packet, clearly marked 'POISON'.

On 15 March Mary Ann Ashford went on trial at Exeter Assizes before Mr Justice Byles. For the prosecution, Mr Kingdon said that 'the prisoner was charged with one of the foulest offences that could be named – that of wilfully, with malice aforethought, poisoning her husband, who of all persons in the world should have been the nearest and dearest to her.' Leading the case for the defence was John Coleridge, who had been elected MP for Exeter the previous year. He told the court that it was unlikely the prisoner, 'however inconsistently she might have acted, would have poisoned her husband like a rat, before the eyes of several persons who had had their suspicions aroused against her. The matter was one of inference and suspicion, but was that sufficient ground upon which to take away the life of a fellow creature?'

The Ashfords' neighbour, Mary Brewer, had been summoned to attend as a witness, but was unable to be present through illness. One of those who took the witness stand was the deceased's brother, Thomas, who confirmed that William was forty-four years of age. He himself was forty: 'my brother was healthy, and a broader, stiffer man than I am.' William Pratt admitted that he had been on very familiar terms with the prisoner, but the relationship was over as he was now engaged. The prisoner had spoken to him about the last will at the time it was made, and when cross-examined, he said he had never known her and her husband quarrel about anything but the will. In view of the Ashfords' altercations in front of other people in the village, this remark seems hard to credit. The document was produced by the executors at the trial and revealed that the deceased had £123, plus effects amounting to £200 or so. Mr Chitty, the Clerk of Arraigns, read several letters written to Mr Pratt by the prisoner, making clear beyond doubt her passion for him, the fact that 'criminal intimacies' had existed between them, and that she had been indifferent towards her husband to the point of callousness.

It took the jury only ten minutes to reach a verdict of guilty. 'Anybody who has heard this evidence cannot entertain the particle of a doubt that you are guilty of that atrocious crime of which the jury has just found you guilty,' remarked the judge. 'You undoubtedly assassinated your own husband by poison, with a view, I fear, of obtaining his little property and returning to the embrace of your paramour.' On being returned to custody under sentence of death, Mary Ann Ashford confessed her guilt and the justice of the verdict. While in her cell at Exeter gaol she tried to strangle herself with a handkerchief, but was prevented just in time by the female warders.

On 18 March her widowed mother-in-law, another Mary Ashford, died at the village poor house, aged seventy-four. Ten days later Mary Ann was hanged at Exeter by William Calcraft. Around 20,000 people were present, it was reported, 'to gratify their morbid curiosity'. Among those were presumably several friends and former clients of her late husband. None of them had ever been in any doubt as to Mary's guilt. Her blatant flaunting of her liaison with William Pratt and her husband's subsequent death in agony told them all they needed to know about her character.

In the normally sleepy little village the event attracted considerable local interest, even to the extent of being immortalised in a local ballad widely circulated on a broadsheet at the time. The verses run as follows:

> Good people all both far and near
> Pray listen unto me
> Mary Ashford she did die
> On Exeter's Gallows tree.
>
> For the murder of her husband dear,
> William Ashford was his name.
> She poisoned him at Clist Honiton,
> And died the death of shame.
>
> In the year 1866
> On March the 28th
> Around the prison of Exeter
> Many hundreds there did wait.
>
> In expectation every moment
> A dreadful sight to see
> A female – Mary Ashford
> Die on the fatal tree.
>
> ''Twas lust and money caused me
> My husband dear to slay
> For another man who worked for him
> I took his life away.
>
> 'May the Lord have mercy on his soul
> I treated him so drear*
> I hope he's gone to the realm above
> My murdered husband dear.'

Mary Ann Ashford was the last woman but one to be hanged in public in England. Two years later the Capital Punishment Amendment Act was passed by parliament, and from August 1868 onwards all executions were privately conducted behind prison walls.

* Word illegible – author's guess.

# 16

# EXTRA DRILL LED HIM TO KILL

## Devonport, 1869

In 1869 William Taylor, aged about twenty-two and a member of the 57th Regiment quartered at Raglan Barracks, Devonport, was like many other young soldiers serving in the British Army. He was married with a wife and baby, and most people who knew him considered he was of good character. In the army he had the small but noteworthy distinction of being awarded a badge for good service. Yet he had from time to time shown signs of mental instability as a child and as an adult. Some of those who had seen him behave peculiarly might not have been altogether surprised that his life was fated to end in tragedy.

On the evening of Tuesday 27 July he committed a serious breach of military discipline by scaling the wall in order to leave his barracks secretly for a few hours. Having won his temporary freedom, he visited a woman's house for, one assumes, the usual kind of assignation. While he was there he met a sailor, who was probably in the house for the same reason. A very merry evening was apparently had by all, not least Taylor, who ended up full of brandy and in no state to return discreetly to barracks that night.

Shortly after getting back the following morning, he was sentenced to be confined to barracks and given extra drill for seven days, which was

*Raglan Barracks, Devonport, in the late nineteenth century.*

*Raglan Barracks, Devonport, Plymouth.* (Courtesy of Tom Bowden)

considered a relatively light punishment. Corporal Arthur Skullin was appointed to see the exercise was carried out, and Taylor was accordingly put on his extra drill with Moses Jaques and Edward Randall, two other defaulters from the same regiment.

On the morning of Saturday 31 July drill was scheduled to start at 6.30. First, Sergeant William Bailey inspected the defaulters and made a remark to Skullin, who asked Bailey if he would inspect each man's kit. Jaques and Randall laid down their knapsacks and passed the test, but Taylor's was found to be empty. He was told that he would be reported to the sergeant-major, and his name sent to the adjutant for further punishment. Taylor said he had got another man's knapsack by mistake, and to give him a second chance Skullin sent him to the barrack-room for his own kit. As Taylor started to walk away, he was called back by Skullin who told him to take his rifle with him.

Lance-Corporal Patrick Burns, of the same regiment, went into the barrack-room at about that time, and noticed Taylor putting on another knapsack. At about 7.20 a.m. Burns returned to the barrack square, and found Skullin drilling all three defaulters together. Each of them, he noticed, had his rifle. The exercises went on for about ten minutes, after which the corporal dismissed the men and went towards his barrack-room. Taylor followed him, and they walked about thirty paces, Taylor being about seven paces behind all the way. Suddenly Taylor halted, took his rifle, put it to his shoulder and fired at Skullin's back. The latter fell immediately to the ground, dead.

When he saw what had happened Burns immediately ran towards Taylor, seized him and took his rifle away. He asked what on earth the soldier thought he was doing, but Taylor made no reply. Burns then took him to the guardroom. At that stage he recalled Taylor having said the previous evening that Corporal Skullin was drilling him 'very hard'.

Taylor was taken to Sergeant Edward Green, who was on duty at the barrack yard. He had heard the shot. Green examined Taylor's rifle, which contained a cartridge case and appeared to be dirty from powder at the muzzle. The barrel was warm, and in Green's mind there was no doubt that it had been recently fired. He handcuffed Taylor, and asked him what had made him do it. Taylor replied that he did not care; it would end his life, and that was what he wanted. 'You don't know everything,' he went on. 'I have a wife and child, and I have behaved very badly to them.' He said nothing more, and Sergeant Green left him in the charge of a sentry.

Police Constable David Shoebert found Taylor in the guardroom, and told him it was his duty to charge him with killing Corporal Skullin. As he was being led to the police station, Taylor said to him, 'It is curious what things come into a man's mind. He was the drill corporal, and he was annoying me the whole morning. I had seven days to barracks. I had not my kit in my knapsack, and he took my name down to report me. It must have been the drill that tempted me.'

George Bell Popplewell, the regiment's surgeon, was summoned to carry out an inspection of the dead man. He found two wounds in the head, one behind the left ear and the other through the left eye. The base of the skull and face on that side were broken, and the brain protruded. The ball had entered the left ear and come out at the left eye, and death must have been instantaneous. Later that day Mr Bone, the Borough Coroner, met a jury at the Stoke Military Hospital, and they then went to Devonport Guildhall where Taylor was formally charged before the Mayor, Dr Rolston. Bone remarked to the jury that the case appeared to him to be as plain as it was melancholy, and a verdict of wilful murder was returned.

Taylor was remanded in custody at Exeter gaol and on 13 August Robert Rainsford, the head warder, took him to Newgate, London, to await trial. The case was considered sufficiently serious to be tried not locally, but at the Central Criminal Court at the Old Bailey. On the journey Taylor made a full confession of his crime. He admitted having escaped from barracks to go out and visit a female companion. He said he had had too much to drink and had no idea what he was doing. Next morning he was ordered to do extra drill, and it only occurred to him on the spur of the moment to shoot the hapless corporal who had been placed in charge of him.

The trial was held on 22 September, the Attorney-General, Sir R.P. Collier, conducting the prosecution on behalf of the Crown, with Mr Molesworth St Aubyn defending. Various personnel from the 57th Regiment, including Colour-Sergeant John English, Lance-Corporal Patrick Burns, John Walsh (the drummer), Privates John Balston and Edward Randall, and Sergeant Bailey, were among those called by the prosecution to give their eye-witness accounts of events immediately before, during and after the killing. Rainsford and Popplewell were also called to corroborate their statements regarding the prisoner's confession and medical details.

For the defence, St Aubyn made much of the likelihood that Taylor was of unsound mind. The question of who was sane and who was not, and where the line was to be drawn 'when reason ceased to assert her sway', he said, 'had been a fascination for mankind from the remotest time'. Witnesses were to be called, St Aubyn went on, to prove that the prisoner's grandmother was mad, that his father had died in a lunatic asylum, and that he himself had exhibited signs of insanity during his boyhood. Only three days before he shot Skullin he had apparently attempted to drown himself at Devonport.

To support his view, St Aubyn quoted from a textbook:

Homicidal mania is commonly defined to be a state of partial insanity accompanied by an impulse to the perpetration of murder. Occasionally the act of murder is perpetrated with great deliberation, and occasionally with all the marks of sanity. Those cases are rendered difficult by the fact that there may be no distinct proof of the existence, past or present, of any disorder of the mind, so that the chief evidence of mental disorder is the act itself.

He proceeded to call several witnesses who could testify to Taylor's recurring mental problems throughout his short life. First was John Cook, a dyer at Kidderminster, who had known Taylor's late grandmother for several years. He averred that she had been completely insane, and could not be left on her own for even an hour. She used to climb a wall stark naked, shouting 'Murder' and 'Fire' for no apparent reason. An uncle was similarly deranged, and had a habit of taking pieces of live coal to set his hair alight for the price of half a pint of ale. The Attorney-General added that the grandmother was never in a lunatic asylum, but lived with her husband, a carpet weaver, until her death. The uncle was an imbecile, who had a well-known drinking problem.

Another witness, Charles Poole, the town crier at Kidderminster, said his wife was an aunt of the prisoner, being Taylor's mother's sister. He had known the prisoner since he was six or seven, and always considered him to be potentially dangerous. On one occasion the lad had been left in charge of Poole's much younger son and threw him down a railway embankment, as a result of which he cut his head badly. His wife Betsy said she had known the prisoner from birth up to about his fourteenth year; once or twice he told her he was going to drown himself. Once he threw himself into a river, and several times he had taken a knife and threatened to cut his throat. He had always been very odd, and once threatened to burn his house down. Her husband, she believed, was afraid of him, and on one occasion sent him to stay with his aunt at Birmingham because they could not put up with him any longer. Taylor's father, she said, died in a lunatic asylum.

The Attorney-General gave evidence that the prisoner had been put to carpet weaving, but would not work. He confirmed that he had often told others he was going to cut his throat, first when he was about thirteen and had been supposed to run an errand for Mrs Poole, but refused and without any warning suddenly turned suicidal.

Thomas Taylor, a carpet weaver at Kidderminster (and no relation), said he had known the prisoner when he was a boy in the Kidderminster Union Workhouse. The other boys used to put him under the pump and douse him with water, after which he would seize a knife or a fork, and the governor would put him in a ward for a time. The prisoner was subject to epileptic fits, and Thomas Taylor had helped in taking his father from the workhouse to a lunatic asylum.

This tendency to mental instability was also borne out by Richard Quigley, a fellow private in the 57th Regiment. He said he had known the prisoner for sixteen months. On 28 July he went with several other soldiers to bathe near Devonport. Without warning Taylor jumped out of his depth and then shouted, 'Save my life!' Quigley and another man promptly swam up to him and prevented him from going under. Later that morning, Taylor told Quigley rather ungraciously that he was not going to thank him, as he might as well be in the water as anywhere else. Another private from the same swimming party reported that Taylor had said in the barrack-room that 'they might as well have let him do it, for he would do it some time or other'. Two other privates from the regiment spoke briefly for the defence, giving additional weight to the argument that Taylor's sanity was in question.

The first witness to be called by the Attorney-General for the prosecution was Hubbard Rose, the Governor of Exeter gaol. He said the prisoner was taken there on 3 August and stayed for ten days, until he was taken to Newgate. He saw him each day, and never noticed anything in his conduct to induce him to believe that Taylor was insane. The prisoner observed the rules faithfully and 'conducted himself in a regular way'.

The chaplain of Exeter gaol, the Revd John Hollins, mentioned seeing and speaking to the prisoner. Once he said the conversation lasted about half an hour, and had reference to the charge against Taylor and the danger he was in. Hollins did not discover any symptom of the prisoner not being in his right mind, though he thought him a rather stupid man. He wrote a letter which the prisoner dictated to him, putting it in witness's language. The subject of the letter seemed rational enough.

The gaol surgeon, Thomas Wilson Caird, and the governor of Newgate, Edmund James Jonas, had both seen the prisoner daily for the last six weeks, and talked to him from time to time, but not longer than five minutes on any occasion. As a prisoner he seemed quiet and well conducted, and showed no signs of insanity. This was substantiated by John Rowland Gibson, the Newgate gaol surgeon, who had had several long interviews with Taylor in order to ascertain the state of his mind. On the subject of crime 'and on other subjects' he always spoke rationally.

On the part of the defence, Mr St Aubyn urged that there was no evidence of malice aforethought on the part of the prisoner, but that with the strong taint of insanity in the family, it might be that the taunts of his corporal and the effects of a sudden paroxysm were too much, 'and his cup of reason overflowed'.

The case for the defence was strong and eloquently argued. In his summing up Attorney-General Collier complimented St Aubyn on his ingenuity, and said how satisfactory it would have been to him if he could have adopted the theory of the defence, for the duty which he and the jury had to discharge was a painful one. However, he could not escape from his duty, which was to impress on them all that in his view the defence of insanity had entirely failed. He dwelt on what had been laid down by the highest authority on the plea of insanity, namely the judges in reply to questions by the House of Lords, and they had said in effect that

> a jury ought to be told in all cases that every man was presumed to be sane, and to possess a sufficient degree of reason to be answerable for his crimes, unless the contrary was proved to their satisfaction; and that to establish a defence on the grounds of insanity it must be clearly proved that at the time of committing the act, the party accused was labouring under such a defect of reason as not to know the quality of the act.

He did not think that the prisoner was mad; the jury had to be satisfied that he was, and that he was so insane that he was unaware of what he was doing. Where, he asked, was the evidence of that? Nobody, he advised, had even suggested that the prisoner had any delusion at the time he committed the crime. The delusion, if any, existed nowhere except in the imagination of Taylor's counsel. He did not know what could countervail such a body of evidence as had been given by the governors, surgeons and chaplains of the prisons in which the prisoner had been confined since committing his crime. While it must be admitted that his father was at one time in an asylum, and madness was in some cases hereditary, so were other afflictions such as gout. A man was not necessarily mad, he said, because his father may have been insane at one time. Supposing, he asked the court, a man was forbidden to make a will because his father had once been in a madhouse; such a theory would be preposterous. The prisoner's grandmother was an eccentric, maybe an alcoholic, but she was never in a lunatic asylum, and she lived with her husband until her death. The uncle too was a drunkard, who had weakened whatever little intellect he ever had. Yet there was no evidence of any insane delusion under which he ever laboured during his life, boy or man.

The jury, he feared, must come to the conclusion that the prisoner had contemplated the crime for some time, and that it was executed with more deliberation and with more malice aforethought than Taylor was willing to confess. He had loaded his rifle some time before he went to drill, and before the corporal was shot. In all probability he loaded it when he went back to fill his knapsack, and it had to be remembered he said to one of the witnesses that he would 'put him out of his mess before night'. It must be assumed that having made such a declaration, Taylor loaded the rifle, and it was probably at this stage that he had the idea of shooting Corporal Skullin. That, Collier submitted, was what the law called malice aforethought.

His learned friend Mr St Aubyn had said the crime was murder or it was nothing, and it would be up to the jury to decide whether it was murder. If the prisoner was held to be mad, it was difficult to say what innocent person was safe from being killed by anyone who could be absolved from blame on grounds of insanity. Had there been fair or reasonable grounds for acquitting the prisoner, Collier should have sincerely rejoiced; but he felt bound to say that he saw no such reason, and he left it to the jury to perform their duty to the public.

In summing up the case for the jury, Mr Justice Brett reminded them first of the solemnity of the duty they had to discharge, and the fact that upon them rested the responsibility of deciding what was the law. If the prisoner was sane at the time, was he guilty of intentional murder? Did he deliberately take aim at the deceased? If he did so, whether it was premeditated or on a sudden impulse, there was nothing which in point of law could reduce the crime to manslaughter. Such an outcome was only possible if they could show that there had been undue provocation on the part of the corporal. While the latter may have acted harshly to the prisoner, this in itself did not provide sufficient grounds for calling the crime manslaughter instead of murder.

It took the jury only five minutes to bring in a verdict of guilty. As the judge put on the black cap and proceeded to pass sentence, he said that the prisoner had committed a grave military offence. He had been properly subjected to a military punishment and it had been the duty of the deceased, Corporal Skullin, to see that he did not evade it. In anger the prisoner had shot him, taking him at a base and cowardly disadvantage. It was to be regretted that such a crime was not so uncommon in the army as it had once been, but it had to be established that whoever was guilty of such an offence would meet with an inevitable doom, and that was the doom of death. Despite assertions made to the contrary, the judge could see no grounds for believing that the convict was not sane at the time of the crime, and he could therefore not escape the ultimate sentence.

Taylor was disowned by his unforgiving relatives, including his wife and young son, and received no visitors in his cell during his last days. On 11 October he was led to the scaffold with faltering steps, sobbing loudly as William Calcraft carried out the full penalty of the law.

# 17

# THE ANGRY BUTCHER

## *Barnstaple, 1877*

William Hussell was well known to the people of Barnstaple as a butcher, and as a heavy drinker who treated his wife Mary abominably, especially when she scolded him for over-indulgence. In the autumn of 1877 he was aged twenty-nine, while she was two years younger. They had four children, Mary, William, Thomas and Edith, of whom the eldest was six years and the youngest a baby of only seven weeks.

On the evening of 1 October Hussell came back to his home at Sanders Cottages, Diamond Street, somewhat the worse for alcohol – and not for the first time. When his wife remonstrated with him he swore at her, threatening to finish her off. Four days later husband and wife were at their shop in the town market until about 8.30 p.m. As usual he had been drinking throughout much of the day, and other traders had heard him quarrelling with her. At the close of business he went back to their home in Diamond Street, but she was afraid to return with him and let him go on first.

*Barnstaple Market, where William and Mary Hussell ran their butcher's shop.*

*The Square, Barnstaple, c. 1900.*

He arrived back to find Emily Dockerty, their fourteen-year-old servant, putting the children to bed. He ordered her to go back to the shop and fetch his wife. Emily did not find Mary Hussell at the shop, but as she came back she met her outside the front door. Mary could hear baby Edith crying and asked Emily to fetch her. William Hussell came outside and asked his wife to come in but she refused, telling him she was afraid to enter because he would only hurt her. Still drunk and very angry, he told her he would not hurt her, then pushed her in, swearing as he did so and telling her she would never go outside the door again alive. She went through the main kitchen into a back kitchen, sat on the stairs to the bedroom, and started breastfeeding Edith. William asked Emily to make Mary some tea, and as he sat down he muttered to himself, 'I will wait until the clock strikes.' Then he pulled a knife from his coat pocket, holding it up to show Mary, saying, 'I have got it ready for you.' 'You can't do it,' she retorted. 'My mother's prayers will be answered for me. I don't take any notice of what you say and when I look at the baby I feel happy.'

He put the knife back in his pocket, but a few moments later he took it out again, mumbling, 'This is what I kill pigs with.' Putting it back in his pocket a second time, he seemed to be hesitating, but then he took it out a third time. 'I will scream murder if you touch me', she said. Emily ran out of the house to the home of Mrs Sanders, a family friend who lived about four doors down. As she ran, she heard Mary screaming 'Murder!' Emily came back, having been gone barely two minutes. On her return she met William who said, 'I have finished her.'

When Emily went indoors, she found Mary lying in the back kitchen on her face. There was blood on the floor and the knife was lying beside her. Emily heard the baby crying but could not see it, and then found it was under Mary. When she asked, 'Mrs Hussell, can I do anything for you?' there was no reply, and she realised her employer's wife was dead.

Emily then went to fetch Elizabeth Sanders, but the next-door neighbour, Eliza Giddy, called to her. She had heard the commotion and screaming, and asked Emily what was going on. When Emily told her she thought Mr Hussell had killed his wife, Mrs Giddy asked her to fetch the baby. When Emily said she could not do so, Mrs Giddy went into the house and took the baby out from under her mother's dead body. Little Edith had a quantity of blood on her nightdress and her arms. A little later Hussell staggered into the Giddys' house and drunkenly told Eliza that he had 'done it', asking her to send for a policeman. He sat down on a chair and collapsed over the table.

Emily had already called Police Constable Thomas Downing, who was on duty at the station. He went into John Giddy's house and found the prisoner still resting his head on the table, saying several times, 'I have done it.' Downing then went next door to verify that Mary Hussell was dead, before heading off to look for Dr Cooke who was not at home. Downing then reported to the station house to tell Superintendent George Longhurst what had happened.

Both men returned to Hussell's house, and the superintendent advised Downing to send for Dr Andrew Fernie. He then helped Sergeant Eddy to take Hussell to the station house. Hussell looked at Eddy, saying, 'My God what have I done, I did not mean to do it, is she dead, tell me.' Eddy told him 'to keep himself quiet and he would let him know presently'. Becoming remorseful, Hussell said, 'I would do sixty years if only I could have her alive.' He struggled violently to get out of Eddy's grasp and became difficult to control, so Eddy called Superintendent Longhurst, who came quickly. Once the prisoner had recovered a little they took him to the police station. He was still very drunk and they had to carry him, while he repeated 'I have done it', and also said, 'I hope she is living.'

Longhurst visited Hussell in his cell at about half-past midnight. He had calmed down by this time and was lying on the bed. He raised himself and sat up before asking if his wife was dead. Longhurst told him she was; 'I then charged him with the wilful murder of his wife. Several times he said he was guilty.'

When Dr Fernie came to the house, he confirmed that Hussell had inflicted two blows on the right breast, one of which penetrated into a large blood vessel below the collarbone. There was also a wound on the left blade-bone, another on the left upper arm, and one on the left side of the face, which passed down to the lower jaw, across the mouth, and through a large blood vessel on the right side of the face.

Hussell was tried at Exeter Assizes on 31 October before Mr Justice Lopes. He pleaded guilty to murder, and though the judge explained to him the nature of the charge and the consequences of his plea, and offered to allow him to withdraw it and be assigned counsel, Hussell would not do so. Among the witnesses called were neighbours, fellow traders and acquaintances who testified to his quarrelsome nature and threats to do away with his wife.

One, John Kingdon, a ship's carpenter, told the court that he had been at the Town Arms Inn in Anchor Lane, Barnstaple, on the afternoon of 5 October when the prisoner came in. After he had downed a glass of ale, Hussell said, 'We must be off from here, her will be after me.' They left together, but could not resist the lure of another watering hole, the Bee Hive in Green Lane, where they stopped for further refreshment. A further walk through the town took them to the Admiral Vernon, where they had several more glasses, Hussell became quarrelsome and took off his coat to fight a man but Kingdon stopped him. Hussell then had a bottle of ginger beer and they were on their way again. It is perhaps needless to add that they went on to visit yet another similar establishment, namely the Bristol Inn, where they ordered yet more ale and spirits, and cooked themselves some fish.

Not surprisingly, Hussell was now very drunk as he boasted to his companions, 'I will do for the bugger.'

He was sentenced to death and hanged on 19 November by William Marwood. Though he walked to the scaffold with a firm step, as the final moment approached he broke down and wept bitterly – as a result of remorse, one would like to assume. Thomas, Hussell's younger son, was adopted by his mother's sister and her husband, while the other three children were sent to an orphanage in Bristol.

# 18

# THE MAN THEY
# COULD NOT HANG

## *Torquay, 1884*

BBritish murderers have achieved notoriety for various reasons. One
Victorian villain has done so for one of the strangest reasons of all: he was
'the man they could not hang'. Three times the executioner tried to carry out
his duty, and three times he failed before his 'client's' sentence was commuted
to life imprisonment. After serving twenty-two years in prison, the villain of
the piece emigrated and lived to a serene old age, dying thirty-eight years after
release and exactly sixty years after he had gone to the gallows. As he wrote

*The Glen, Babbacombe, Torquay.* (From *Executioner*, Stewart P. Evans, Sutton Publishing)

and published his memoirs shortly after release in 1908, the story and his thoughts on subsequent events are uniquely well documented.

John Henry George Lee was born at Abbotskerswell in August 1864, the son of a farmer. His parents, John and Mary, had already had a daughter, Amelia, and Mary also had an illegitimate daughter from a previous relationship. This girl, Elizabeth Harris, was raised by her grandparents in Kingsteignton. At the age of fifteen John became a junior servant at The Glen, a seaside house at Babbacombe, Torquay, which belonged to Emma Keyse, an elderly spinster. During boyhood he had always been fascinated by the sea, and despite parental opposition he joined the Royal Navy in October 1879. He proved a promising cadet, and just over a year later he was awarded an Admiralty Prize for good progress. However, any hopes of promotion and foreign travel were dashed when he was stricken with pneumonia at the age of eighteen, and after a spell at the Royal Naval Hospital in Plymouth, where his illness was at one stage thought to be life-threatening, he was invalided out of the service. He found it hard to settle down to civilian life, and within a year he had had three jobs, none of which he really enjoyed.

By the end of 1882, thanks partly to a reference from Miss Keyse, he was employed as a servant by Colonel Edward Brownlow in Torquay. Six months into this post, he took advantage of the colonel's absence on holiday by stealing some of the family silver and trying to sell it to a pawnbroker in Devonport. He was arrested, found guilty and sentenced to six months' imprisonment in Exeter gaol. Before his release the chaplain received a letter from Miss Keyse, explaining that she had always found the prisoner honest, truthful and obedient. If Lee was prepared to give her an undertaking as to his future good conduct, she would gladly employ him again as her gardener.

He accepted the position and returned to work for her in the spring of 1884. Meanwhile, she assured him she would do what she could to find him a more remunerative position elsewhere. As he now had a criminal record, Lee would find it difficult to obtain employment with anyone else, but Miss Keyse planned to put The Glen on the market and hoped to place her small number of devoted servants with other households as soon as she reasonably could. It may or may not have been a coincidence that at this time Lee began to do less and less around the house and garden. He remained impervious to her speaking to him on the subject. As she was reluctant to dismiss him, Miss Keyse told him instead that she would reduce his weekly wages from 2s 6d to 2s. He became surly, argumentative with everyone and made no secret of his lack of respect for 'the old woman'. Soon after this he became engaged to a local dressmaker, Kate Farmer, but realised he was not earning enough to support a wife. Frustrated by his lack of prospects, in October he briefly broke off the engagement, but Kate entreated him to reconsider, and they were reunited.

On 28 October Miss Keyse found a buyer for her estate at an auction in London. Later that day she paid her servants their quarterly salaries, owed in arrears, and Lee was furious to discover that she had carried out her intention to reduce his wages. She still assured him she would ask the new owners of the house to keep him on, but he evidently took the attitude that if he was receiving less money, he was obliged to work less hard. The atmosphere at The Glen became increasingly volatile.

Less than three weeks later, in the small hours of 15 November, the maid, Jane Neck, took Miss Keyse her nightly cup of cocoa and went to bed as usual. At some stage within the next two or three hours, Miss Keyse got up, went out into the hall and was savagely attacked. Her assailant bludgeoned her skull, slit her throat and then dragged her body into the dining-room where he attempted to burn it. He also lit other fires indoors. Between 3 and 4 a.m. the cook, Lee's half-sister Elizabeth Harris, woke up, smelled burning, and got up to rouse Jane and her sister Eliza, the only other servants in the house apart from Lee. When he appeared in response to her frightened cries, he was partly dressed. The house was full of smoke and he led her downstairs.

Coastguards and fishermen were summoned to help put out the blaze. On investigation it was discovered that five separate fires had been started in different places in the house, which smelled strongly of paraffin. In the hall was a pool of blood, and in the dining-room lay the body of Miss Keyse. Everyone thought at first that she had succumbed to the effects of smoke, and they were astonished to find that the cause of her death was something very different. The extent of her injuries was immediately apparent; newspapers had been spread around her body and set alight but had merely smouldered.

A window in the dining-room was broken, and when questioned Lee admitted he had smashed it. He had cut his arm, he said, while trying to let smoke out of the house. It was then realised that his hand had touched Elizabeth's nightdress before he broke the window, which explained the bloodstains on her garment, and more blood was found on the oil-can containing the paraffin used to light the fire. A towel and knife, which Lee kept to use for gardening, and a pair of trousers, all stained and smelling of paraffin, were also found in his quarters. The police superintendent warned him that as he was the only man in the house, he would be 'apprehended on suspicion' of murder.

An inquest was held at the town hall in St Marychurch and Lee was brought before Torquay magistrates. On 3 December, at Torquay police station, he was formally charged with the murder of Miss Keyse and committed for trial at Exeter Assizes.

Miss Keyse had been much loved and respected by local residents, and there was considerable indignation against the man whom they believed had killed her so callously. The vicar of St Marychurch preached a sermon to his congregation on Sunday 23 November, dwelling on the tragedy that had befallen them as a community, and how terrible it was that 'the one who served God so well should have fallen the victim of a heartless, cold-blooded, stealthy murder'.

The trial began on 2 February 1885 before Mr Justice Manisty, with Mr A. Collins and Mr Vigor conducting the case for the prosecution, and Mr Molesworth St Aubyn for the defence. Maintaining his innocence throughout the three-day proceedings, Lee pleaded not guilty. Among witnesses for the prosecution were Elizabeth Harris and a postman, both of whom said they had heard Lee make threats against Miss Keyse. The postman said that Lee had vowed to 'put an end to someone in the house before long', and that if she 'did not soon get him a better place she would wish she had'. Harris repeated similar remarks, and said that Lee had threatened several times to burn down the house, especially after Miss Keyse had told him she was going to reduce his wages. At the time Harris was expecting a child, and she gave birth to a daughter, Beatrice, in the Newton Abbot workhouse six weeks later. The father was never named, but there was speculation that Beatrice was the result of an incestuous relationship between Harris and her half-brother. This was possibly no more than hearsay on the part of those who had already made up their minds that a fiend capable of beating an elderly lady to death could be responsible for anything.

The case against Lee looked reasonably straightforward, and it took the jury only forty minutes to reach a verdict of guilty. The judge told the prisoner that he had 'maintained a calm appearance' throughout the case, which did not surprise him. Even so, he had been 'found guilty of the murder upon evidence so clear to my mind, and so absolutely conclusive, that I am sorry to say I cannot entertain a doubt of the correctness of their verdict'. Lee was strangely unmoved by the verdict. 'The reason, my Lord,' he answered, 'why I am so calm and collected is because I trust in my Lord, and He knows I am innocent.' The *Western Morning News* thought otherwise, noting on 5 February that it was 'difficult to contemplate without a shudder the guilt which was brought home with absolute conclusiveness against him'. *The Times* was equally virulent in its condemnation of the prisoner, thundering in similar vein that 'the man who ought to have been her protector slew her in a barbarous and fiendish fashion, and added to his crime by endangering the lives of his three fellow servants, one of whom was his own sister'.

According to usual custom, there was a period of three clear Sundays between the judge's pronouncement of the death sentence and the execution itself. In his memoirs, Lee wrote that those three weeks were generally more terrible than the actual execution itself, but not in his case; he felt relieved because he knew what to expect. When the governor came to his cell to tell him the date fixed for the execution, he turned round and smiled. The governor told him in a very shocked voice that it was 'nothing to laugh at'.

On 23 February Lee went to the gallows at Exeter gaol. Next day the *Dartmouth & Brixham Chronicle* told its readers that 'the culprit died easily'. It can only be assumed that the reporter did his work earlier that morning and took the rest of the day off, for the culprit did not die easily; in fact, he did not die at all. What happened was one of the most bizarre episodes ever recorded in the history of British justice.

During the night, Lee had written farewell letters to his parents and sister, received the Last Sacrament, and settled down to what should have been his final rest on earth, 'the last before the long, peaceful sleep of death'. He dreamed that he was on the scaffold and heard the bolt drawn three times but it failed to operate. On the morning of 23 February the Revd John Pitkin entered the cell, and stayed with Lee until the executioner, James Berry, arrived to pinion him and prepare him for the end.

Lee walked without assistance to the correct place beneath the beam, his legs were fastened, the rope was adjusted around his neck and the white cap drawn over his head. While the chaplain finished intoning the service for the burial of the dead, Berry pulled the lever, which should have freed the bolts on the trapdoors beneath the prisoner. Instead of the sharp jerk that should have launched Lee into eternity, the boards merely quivered. Berry tugged the lever again, thinking he had not pulled hard enough, while the attendant warders each used a foot to give added weight to the drop. Again, nothing happened. With the rope still around his neck and the hood still over his head, Lee was quickly escorted away as the warders set about searching for any obstruction that might have affected the working of the apparatus. Berry tested everything quickly and found that the doors were in working order. Lee was brought forward again and the chaplain repeated the last sentences of the service. Again Berry pulled the lever, but again the equipment failed to work.

It was six minutes since the procession had walked from the prison. Displaying astonishing fortitude and self-control, Lee stood as the rope was removed from around his neck and the white cap from his head, and he was escorted back to the main part of the prison. The structure on the scaffold was carefully examined and tested, and Lee was brought out for a third attempt. As Berry pulled the lever once more, the structure quivered visibly – but the trapdoors remained firmly closed. Twenty minutes had elapsed since the first attempt. Lee was led back to the prison once more, and the increasingly embarrassed prison staff brought saws, chisels and other tools in an effort to make the equipment work. They were forestalled when the sheriff, acting on his own authority, ordered a stay of execution pending instructions from the Home Secretary, Sir William Harcourt. As Berry returned home to await his next job, having been paid his fee in full despite having failed to discharge his duty, local and national newspapers rang with the headline that would be eternally associated with the day's events – 'THE MAN THEY COULD NOT HANG'.

Lee had apparently taken this turn of events with equanimity. If he is to be believed – and naturally it is easier to be wise after the event – he seems to

*James Berry's lantern slide depicting his attempted execution of John Lee.* (© Madame Tussaud, from *Executioner*, Stewart P. Evans, Sutton Publishing)

have had a touching faith in his dream that he would survive the attempts to put him to death. His Christian beliefs, he was sure, had sustained him. When he wrote to his sister twenty-four hours later, he told her that 'it was the Lord's will' that he should not die at the time appointed by man.

Newspaper reports of his being on the verge of collapse were credible enough, but he denied them. The cap on his head, he said, was slowly smothering him, so he tried to push it off by bending his head down and raising his manacled hands. The officials who saw him thought he was on the point of fainting. Once he was back in his cell, he proved that his appetite had not been affected. The doctor told him he could eat anything he wanted, so he promptly asked for a second breakfast of ham and eggs, to be followed by a beefsteak with half a pint of port for dinner. As he had already had one breakfast, not even the superhuman achievement of besting the hangman's noose three times in a row was enough to qualify him for a second sitting and he had to wait until the following morning.

The apparatus had been thoroughly examined and tested on the previous Saturday, and its failure to work was never satisfactorily explained. The main theory advanced, but not conclusively proved, was that heavy rainfall on the Saturday night had caused the woodwork to swell.

*John Lee.*

Even Queen Victoria was horrified enough to intervene personally in the case. Within hours she had heard the extraordinary news, and from Windsor Castle she sent a telegraph to Harcourt expressing her horror at 'the disgraceful scenes at Exeter' at the execution:

> Surely he cannot *now* be executed? It would be *too* cruel. Imprisonment for life seems the only alternative. But since this new executioner has taken it in hand there have been several accidents. Surely some safe and certain means could be devised which would make it quite sure. It should be of *iron* not wood, and such scenes must not recur.

For a month Lee was given to understand that his stay of execution was no more than that, and not until March was he informed that his death sentence would be commuted to life imprisonment. Penal servitude for life, the governor of Exeter prison told him, would mean twenty years, though Harcourt had recommended that he should never be released.

Although (or perhaps because) his defence was thought to have been rather half-hearted, Mr Molesworth St Aubyn was cheered by this turn of events. On 24 February he wrote to Pitkin that he was among those who had never been fully satisfied as to Lee's guilt: 'What a marvellous thing if he turns out to be innocent!'

But if Lee was not the murderer of Miss Keyse, who was? It was said that Elizabeth Harris had a lover, a man prominent in London society, who sometimes slipped into the kitchen at night after Miss Keyse had gone to bed. On the night in question, she came down to speak to Lee, who slept in the pantry, and when she opened the kitchen door and saw what was happening, she recognised the man and fainted from shock. The man feared scandal, killed her, started the fire and bribed Lee handsomely to take the blame, assuring him that he had friends in high places who would somehow ensure that the gallows would not work.

Initially after the failed execution Lee had to spend a short period in solitary confinement, which in his case was at Pentonville for three months and then Wormwood Scrubs for another four. After this he was transferred to Portsmouth prison, where he was employed making hammocks and working on the construction of new docks in the seaport. He then spent six and a half years in the prison laundry. When Portsmouth prison was closed in 1892, he was moved to Portland, where inmates worked in the local quarries and stone-cutting sheds. For some time he was punishment orderly and had an exemplary record for good behaviour.

Each year he petitioned the Home Secretary to release him, protesting his innocence and citing his ordeal on the scaffold as extenuating grounds in his favour. For twenty years he was to be disappointed. However, in 1906 a Liberal government came to power, and the new Home Secretary, Herbert

Gladstone – whose father, William Ewart Gladstone, was Prime Minister when Lee had begun his sentence – reviewed the case and decided that it was in Lee's best interests to set him free. Imprisonment for life, he wrote in a letter to one of his under-secretaries, would inevitably mean 'mental and bodily decay', and if he was to be allowed out, 'it is best to do it at once'.

The Home Office agreed that Lee should be allowed to sell his story by writing his memoirs, something which officials believed would be no more than a passing sensation. Lee's notoriety, it was assumed, would be a short-lived phenomenon and he would soon be forgotten. It was decided that he should be freed on licence, among the conditions set being that he should 'not habitually associate with notoriously bad characters, such as reputed thieves and prostitutes', nor 'lead an idle and dissolute life, without visible means of obtaining an honest livelihood'. Most important of all, a clause was added which forbade him from trading on his notoriety by taking part in any public performances, delivering any lectures or speeches, or exhibiting 'himself at any meeting, assembly or place of entertainment'. The previous government had been alarmed by rumours of his imminent release, and not surprisingly also by an offer from the owner of a music hall in Middlesex for Lee and Berry, the hangman who had failed to kill him, to appear on stage together for a fee of £100 per week. Trying to create a theatrical double act out of such a macabre event was surely stretching the bounds of good taste a little too far.

Berry, who resigned his position as executioner in 1892 after a few other botched executions (in one the murderer was decapitated by the rope), had displayed a wonderful talent for opportunism. Having executed 134 men and women during his eight-year career, he publicly came out against the death penalty, not only publishing his memoirs but also embarking on lucrative tours, lecturing on his experiences in a talk entitled 'From Public Executioner to Preacher of the Gospel'. During his period of office he had sold to a Nottingham publican the complete length of rope with which he tried to hang Lee. For some years afterwards he charged buyers 1s for a piece of the noose allegedly used on Lee – though the genuine article had long since been elsewhere.

Lee walked out of prison a free man in the utmost secrecy on 18 December 1907. He was escorted by a chief warder and his wife, who were going to spend Christmas in Torquay. Lee's father had died five years previously, but his mother was still living at Abbotskerswell, and he chose to pay her a surprise visit. Somehow rumours had preceded him, and several pressmen had gathered to wait outside the family home. He had barely arrived before editors were competing for the rights to print his story. On 29 December 1907 the mass circulation *Lloyd's Weekly News* began a series of episodes on the murder, Lee's experiences on the scaffold and his years in prison. The deal was said to have gained him £240, a handsome sum which precluded any urgent need to look for work.

In January 1909 Lee married Jessie Bulleid at a secret ceremony at Newton Abbot. One year later she gave birth to their son, also named John. Thirteen months later, in February 1911, he abandoned Jessie – who was expecting a second child – and their son when he sailed for New York with a woman whom he described as his wife. This was Adelina Gibbs, whom he met while they were working together at a public house in London and whom he probably never married but stayed with for the rest of his life.

A silent film based on his story, *The Man They Could Not Hang*, was made in Australia in 1912. Because of its poor technical quality, it was shelved by the producer, who passed it on to one of his employees. The man thought this was too good an opportunity to miss. Within a few years, he and an associate had enjoyed considerable success by showing it in cinemas throughout Australia and New Zealand. An expanded version was produced in 1921 and shown widely throughout Britain, and it was said, though never proved, that Lee made personal appearances at some of the cinemas concerned.

The rest of Lee's life is shrouded in some mystery. John Lee is a common name, and it is probable that others tried to pass themselves off as 'the man they could not hang'. His mother died in 1918 and ten wreaths were laid at her grave, but none of them on behalf of her son. One report says that he emigrated to Australia and died in Melbourne the same year as his mother. Another suggests that he went to Canada and died in an unspecified part of the country in 1921. According to another, he stayed in or came back to England, and took over a furniture shop in Plymouth in about 1920, shortly before committing suicide.

The most likely version seems to be that he and Adelina stayed in America and settled in Milwaukee. They had a daughter, Evelyn, who was employed as a maid but died in October 1933 at the age of nineteen after suffocating from naphtha fumes while cleaning her employer's apartment. Assuming this was the same John Lee, then he was still alive for many years after those scenes on the scaffold at Exeter were but a distant memory. On 19 March 1945, at the age of eighty, he succumbed to a heart attack at his home. Adelina survived him by twenty-three years, dying at the age of ninety-four on 9 January 1969.

# 19

# THE RIVERKEEPER
# AND THE POACHERS

*Tiverton, 1887*

Archibald Reed, a former soldier, was a stonemason by trade. In 1887 he was thirty-seven years old, and he and his wife, Mary Ann, to whom he had been married for three years, lived at Water Lane, Tiverton. It was an appropriate address for a man who was employed by the Tiverton Fishing Association as a riverkeeper. Described as being of medium height, squarely built, muscular, 'a most respectable character', he was also known to be 'somewhat taciturn and reserved, and fearless in carrying out his duty'. Apart from a slightly stiff left arm as a result of an accident some years before, he was perfectly fit and healthy. Conscientious to a fault, he had a reputation as 'a terror to poachers by reason of his firmness', and although he had only

*Water Lane, Tiverton. (© James Cosgrave)*

been employed for six months in this capacity, by the end of July 1887 he had already brought several miscreants to justice. Throughout the area he was hated and feared, and had at least once been openly threatened with violence in the course of his duty.

Knowing that he could be at risk from potential assailants, on the afternoon of 29 July he had an interview with the chairman of the Fishing Association, who promised him that sometime in the future he would be given assistance so that a longer stretch of the water could be controlled more effectively. That evening Reed went for a drink at the Country House Inn with George Davey, a gamekeeper employed by Sydney Stern of Collipriest House, an imposing residence by the River Exe. The latter warned him that a gang of poachers was liming the river, and large quantities of fish were likely to be stolen or killed in the process. He gave Reed a description of the men whom he had been following and watching at a distance only days before, and said he had heard they were going to lime Lock's Pitt, probably that night.

'We'll have them between us,' Reed vowed. 'Very well, I shall be out all night.' Keen to catch the poachers and aware that such a task would be impossible if Davey was on his own, Reed then asked if he knew anybody who could be relied on to help. He himself knew forty or fifty, but was not sure he could trust them. Davey said he could not think of anyone, but would offer what help he could.

From the inn Reed went home, and in the course of conversation with his wife he mentioned he was going to have help, as four poachers – at least one of whom he knew by name – were expected later. As reinforcements were not guaranteed, she expressed fears for his safety. 'What would you be against four, Archie?' she asked him. He told her that he would leave them until they were down at the water, then go up and say to them, 'Now what little game are you at?' When she warned him that they would surely murder him, he said that if there was any violence he would not hesitate to knock them on the head. 'They'll run, they like their lives too well,' he assured her. 'If I don't die before I am murdered by others I shall live to a good age.' She urged him to take a whistle to make the poachers believe that other keepers were about, a suggestion which he disregarded. He started from home as usual at around 11 p.m., and on leaving said he did not expect to be back until 7 a.m. next day. Though she had her doubts at first, Mary Ann was not unduly alarmed when he did not return at his usual hour.

At about 1.30 a.m. the dogs at Collipriest started to bark and the caretaker heard them, but he could not see any intruders and did not realise anything unusual had happened. All became clear a few hours later. Shortly before 4 a.m. Davey, coming back from a walk in the woods, passed down the riverbank, keeping his eyes open carefully, but he did not notice anything was wrong. After that he walked on to Pitt Farm and went around the coverts, returning by Collipriest Walk. At about 6 a.m. he saw something odd in the river at a stretch just outside Tiverton on the main road to Exeter, a few inches from the opposite bank. Finding it was the body of a man face downwards in the water, he called the police and Constable Raymond came along to see. They waded across the river, which was for the most part only a few inches deep.

Davey's discovery confirmed his worst fears. It was the badly mutilated body of Reed, his face disfigured with stabs and cuts, and his throat cut from ear to ear. On his left cheek were three deep wounds, and his left ear was hanging by just a piece of skin. The fingers of the left hand were cut to the bone in seven or eight places, while both hands were punctured and lacerated all over. Such injuries were indicative of a desperate struggle. Reed had evidently put up a fight against his attackers, for one of them must have been wearing a blue spotted tie which was left on the ground, stamped with blood. Two pipes, a trout, a piece of rope with a noose at one end, an open pocket knife stained with blood, a blue striped handkerchief, a pair of scissors and a lead pencil were also found under the trees in the adjoining field. A wall about 2 feet above road level skirted the field, and over it were found Reed's hat and broken walking stick. Three large pools of blood were discovered under the larger tree, and leading from these to the river, a distance of about 10 yards, was a trail of blood 4 inches wide. This suggested that the body had been dragged by the legs and then rolled down the bank into the river, but there was not enough water to cover it. The water at this particular point was stagnant, and small pools of blood still remained for several hours after the attack took place. On a patch of rising ground near the road a streak of blood was still visible in the grass where the murderer, or one of them – it was immediately thought that a gang had been responsible – must have wiped his hands. Hair of two distinct colours was found on the spot, some of it matching Reed's own, but some much greyer and presumably from an older man. As the ground was so dry, no footprints had been left in the field, but there were three in the road, and these were taken in plaster by the police.

Raymond and Davey took Reed's body in a handcart to his home at Water Lane. When told that what she had dreaded had come to pass, Mary Ann, prostrate with grief, was taken to a neighbour's house to be comforted.

Superintendent Crabb of the borough police sent telegrams to all the other police stations in the county, and despatched a constable to visit the surrounding districts. The houses of certain notorious poachers were searched, and several men were questioned. Particular suspicion fell on Mr Western, who lived in Bickleigh. The former navvy had previously worked for the Exe Valley Railway and the sewerage works. He had suffered various injuries in the past, including fractures to both arms, and was well known as a regular poacher, with a string of charges for 'murderous assaults' to his name. Although he was quite elderly, only two months earlier he had been convicted of disorderly conduct, and Reed was one of the witnesses against

*The River Exe from Tiverton, where Archibald Reed patrolled regularly as a riverkeeper, and where he met a violent death at the hands of persons unknown in July 1887.*

him. Thereafter he had been heard to threaten Reed in public. He bore several recent wounds, including a blackened right eye and a left hand cut in two places, but he explained them by saying he had fallen over a hedge a few hours previously. When he was examined by the doctor, the wounds were thought to have been inflicted only about three days earlier. But he was not detained, and after the doctor's statement he was at liberty to go.

Several people in the area were certain Western was responsible for Reed's murder, and despite a lack of firm evidence, there was some criticism of the police for letting him go so quickly. When someone accused him to his face of being involved, he retorted, 'How could I tackle a strong man like Reed when I have had both my arms broken?' He was not one of the men Archibald Reed had mentioned to his wife; on the contrary, Reed had told her that Western was too old to do him any harm.

Crabb had several clues and, reported the press with confidence, 'there is hardly any doubt that the murderers will not remain much longer at large'. An inquest was opened at Tiverton Town Hall on 1 August and adjourned until the following week. Among the witnesses called to give evidence was the widow, who had great difficulty in speaking at times because she kept breaking down. She told the coroner that her husband had been promised

*Tiverton Town Hall.* (© Hannah Lindsey-Clark)

help that night, but it never materialised. Davey gave a faithful version of events from his meeting with the deceased in the inn to his discovery of the body early the next morning. PC Raymond and several other policemen also gave evidence. Two had spoken during the previous few days to Reed, who told them of the increase in poaching activity and said that he wanted 'to drop them if I can'.

The findings were obvious. At the last day of the inquest, the jury declared that Reed 'was found wilfully murdered on the morning of 30 July, but that at present there is no evidence to prove by whom'.

Despite extensive investigations during the next few weeks, nobody was ever convicted or even arrested for the murder. Mary Ann Reed died in May 1922 with the case still unsolved.

# 20

# ATROCITY AT PETER TAVY

*Peter Tavy, 1892*

Rarely did anything disturb the peace of Peter Tavy, a small close-knit village about 3 miles from Tavistock. But the gruesome events of a winter's evening late in 1892 temporarily shattered that peace in no uncertain fashion.

Among the families who lived in the community were the Williamses, the Doidges and the Rowes. William Williams, the eighteen-year-old son of the village miller, had become thoroughly smitten with Emma Doidge, a girl of seventeen, whose family lived at Cox Tor Farm. As well as farming at the

*Peter Tavy Mill, the home and workplace of William Williams and his family.*

property, her father John was a churchwarden. For a while Emma was happy to spend time with William, but before long she found his constant attention tiresome. He wrote her a couple of letters begging her to take him back, but she replied with brief notes, telling him firstly that she could only look on him as a brother, and secondly that she did not want him to communicate with her any more. He was nothing if not persistent, and he still hoped that she would eventually change her mind. Soon he became increasingly jealous of any other young men whom he thought might be getting too friendly with Emma, and when it seemed that she was becoming rather fond of William Rowe, whose family lived at Lucy Cottage, he decided to act.

On 8 November Williams went to Tavistock to buy a revolver for 5s from Samuel Blanchard, who ran an ironmonger's shop in Brook Street. Blanchard knew Williams well, as he had often bought rifle cartridges at the shop. In spite of the fact that his trade might suffer slightly as a result, Blanchard had recently discussed with Williams the possibility that he might make his own cartridges to save money. When Blanchard asked him why he wanted the revolver, Williams said that he wanted to shoot a dog. He also asked Blanchard if the weapon 'would kill across the street', and was told that it would. Despite this conversation, not for one moment did it apparently cross the vendor's mind that his customer had any more sinister motive in mind.

Williams had the forethought to keep his weapon carefully concealed about his person, and on Sunday 13 November he put it in his coat pocket before going to attend evening service at St Peter's Church. All the families were pillars of the local church: William Rowe worked the bellows for his organist father, Joseph; Emma Doidge and her younger sister, Elizabeth, sang in the church choir; William Williams himself was one of the bellringers, and had taken his part in ringing that afternoon.

Emma's brother, also called William, was a regular churchgoer too. Some of the villagers thought that he attended services mainly so he could keep an eye on her and shield her from Williams's unsolicited attentions, but as the family was so committed to church activities, he would almost certainly have taken his place in the pews each Sunday anyway. After the service, Williams walked over to William Rowe, and evidently got the message that his presence was unwelcome. 'I'll knock your block off,' Williams said to Emma. 'You shan't touch her while I'm here,' William immediately told him. As Williams left, he was heard to mutter under his breath that somebody would 'fall tonight'. He also mumbled something to the effect that as they all had their Sunday clothes on, he would wait until the morning and then fight William Doidge.

As usual, William Rowe, Emma and her brother were among a large group of young people going home from church together in the direction of Cox Tor Farm. Others in the group included Emma's sister Elizabeth, and Annie, daughter of local farmer William Mudge. These girls, like Emma, all belonged to the choir. On this occasion, William Rowe and Emma had been delayed for a few moments because the vicar, the Revd Dr Bryant, had left his umbrella behind at the church and asked William if he would mind going back for it. When they came out with the umbrella, little did they know that Williams had gone ahead and was hiding behind a tree in Creedy Lane, waiting for them. As William Doidge was entering their house, Elizabeth was just behind him. She heard four shots. They walked back down the road, about 500 yards, and could not believe what they saw.

While William Rowe and Emma Doidge were on their way home not far behind, Williams had jumped out at them and taken the revolver out of his pocket. A terrified William Rowe tried to run away but was shot in the head and fell to the ground unconscious as Emma tried to go to Sowtontown Farm for help. Williams seized her and she struggled to get away from him, tearing her jacket badly in the process. He fired at her and she was killed instantly. When their bodies were found, William Rowe's was about 12 yards in front of Emma's. Next Williams turned the gun on himself, and the bullet struck him in the head but did no more than knock him off his feet. He tried to shoot himself again and this time the bullet took out one of his eyes.

After taking the service, Dr Bryant was sitting by the fire in his drawing room, reading. He was roused by the general commotion. A grief-stricken Mr Rowe ran in to tell him that his son and Emma Doidge had just been shot. The vicar had prepared Emma for confirmation, and this grim news came almost on the exact anniversary of the day that she had been confirmed. He paid a visit to Cox Tor Farm to offer his condolences.

By this time Emma's father had reached Creedy Lane, with Mr Mudge from Sowtontown Farm. The police had already been called to the scene of the crimes, and after they had concluded their investigations, the distraught Mr Doidge took his daughter's body to Cox Tor Farm in his trap, while Mr Mudge took the still unconscious William Rowe to Lucy Cottage. Dr Broderick went to Cox Tor and confirmed that Emma was dead. Next he visited Lucy Cottage, but after examining William Rowe, he sadly told his parents that he could hold out no hope. William lingered until 9 a.m. the next day and died without regaining consciousness.

Meanwhile, on the Sunday evening Williams bled profusely from his self-inflicted wounds as he staggered across the fields to the bank of the River Tavy and threw himself in. Either his attempt to drown himself proved as futile as the suicide bid with his revolver, or else he had second thoughts. After floating some distance downstream, he hauled himself out and staggered to a house at Harford Bridge, the home of George Doidge, a mason, who was not related to Emma's family. Mr Doidge was awakened about half an hour after midnight by the sound of loud knocking at his door. At first his wife thought it must be a passing drunk, but he went downstairs to investigate.

Though he knew Williams, at first he did not recognise the dishevelled figure with blood pouring from his head. When he asked Williams what the matter was, the latter said, 'Go and tell my father where I am. He will know all about it by this time. This is not the worst of it yet.' One of Doidge's daughters made a cup of tea for Williams, who drank it but refused to give any explanation for his condition. A little later, Williams's father and a policeman arrived at Doidge's house at the same time, and he was taken to Tavistock Cottage Hospital for treatment. When Dr Broderick extracted the bullet from his neck, he compared it with those taken from the heads of the victims and found they corresponded. At the hospital on Monday Williams said all he wanted to do was to see his parents. After that, the doctors could do what they pleased with him.

An inquest into both deaths was held on Tuesday 15 November at Cox Tor Farm. Among those present were Mr R.R. Dodd, the County Coroner; Mr T. Martin Rogers, the foreman; Superintendent Nicholls and Sergeant Pike, representing the police; Dr Bryant; Mr Holmes, Emma's maternal grandfather; and her father. After the formal identification of her body, they went to the village, passing the spot where the deed had taken place. Traces of blood were still to be seen and a large clot under a piece of timber marked the spot where Emma had died. After pausing at the Peter Tavy Inn to register their names, they went to Lucy Cottage for the formal identification of William Rowe's body. His father Joseph was there, and though he had maintained his composure till then, at the ceremony he collapsed, overcome with grief, crying out, 'My poor boy! My poor boy!' On their return to the inn, a unanimous decision was taken to adjourn the inquest until all the evidence had been gathered and post-mortem reports finalised by Dr Broderick.

On 16 November Police Constable Callard visited Williams at the cottage hospital. Mr Williams later came to see his son. 'Father, will you tell me the sense and truth of what has happened?' the young man asked. Mr Williams told him that William Rowe and Emma Doidge were going to be buried. 'Then they are dead?' his son asked him, still evidently a little confused. Then William Williams made a statement which the policeman recorded:

Father, I loved her dearly and it is all through the love and affection I had for her, and the provocation that I have received from other young men of the village that has led me to do what I have. It has been playing on my mind for the last four or five weeks, and, do whatever I could, I could not drive it off. They have trifled with me terribly. My intention to her was good, and I knew one or two others that used to go home with her, and that troubled me terribly. They have trifled with me so long until it has come to this. I have often had something to drink lately, thinking that would ease my mind, but no, it was all no good. Then I got to a terrible pitch, that I thought I would buy a revolver.

*The grave of William Rowe, his parents and sister at St Peter's Church, Peter Tavy.*

He went on to say that after he had bought the weapon he was afraid of it, as he had never seen one before. In order to try it out he fired at some birds, but did not think he succeeded in hitting any. 'I was not sure exactly whether it would kill or not. My mind was not easy then; I could not sleep at night; I was always thinking about it.'

A double funeral was held at the church on 17 November. The coffins were covered with floral tributes, and about 700 people attended. Both victims had been well-respected members of much-loved families who had long been known to the community, and many people at the church were weeping, still stunned at the horror of the incident which seemed so hard to comprehend.

Two days later, at 10 a.m., the inquest was resumed and concluded at the village school. The causes of both deaths were formally recorded, and a report on Williams's condition was also given. The remains of his wounded eye had been removed, and his bullet injuries were healing, though he was still in hospital and would probably not be well enough to be discharged for at least a month. Dr Bryant gave him what was described as 'a good character

*St Peter's Church, Peter Tavy.*

reference', though this was contested by some of the villagers, who said – perhaps with hindsight – that he had always had a shifty appearance which did not invite trust.

Yet another untimely death was reported in the village that week. A friend of the Williams family, Mr Maddock, a man of thirty with a wife and small child, called at the house to express his sympathy to the parents. After leaving, he had only walked a few yards when he collapsed with a burst blood vessel. He was only saved from falling into the stream by the quick-witted presence of another man nearby. A policeman took him home just before he expired.

Williams recovered more quickly from his wounds than everyone had anticipated. Though still not completely better, he was allowed out of hospital in time for a two-day trial before the magistrates at Tavistock Guildhall on 29 and 30 November. Such was the interest in the case that the crowd gathering outside before the investigation began was estimated to have been enough to fill the hall ten times over. When the doors were opened to the public, after the magistrates had taken their seats and the prisoner was in the dock, there was such an unseemly scramble for the best seats that the police had to restore order and stop the fighting that broke out. Many of those who had to be excluded for lack of room then blockaded the doorway, and business was delayed so that silence and decorum could be restored.

That Williams's recovery was not complete soon became clear. He was still so weak that he was allowed to sit. He had to be helped in and out of the dock by policemen, and he wore a flesh-coloured shade over his face where the right eye had been. Throughout the hearing he betrayed no emotion, but kept pressing his hands against his head in pain. On the second day of the trial he fainted, and the hearing had to be suspended until he came round. After the trial he was taken back to the hospital and on the following day – 1 December, his nineteenth birthday – he was remanded at Exeter gaol.

On 9 March 1893 he appeared at the Lent Assizes in Exeter before Mr Justice Lawrance, charged with 'feloniously, wilfully and of malice aforethought killing and murdering William Frederick Rowe and Emma Holmes Doidge at Peter Tavy'. The Hon. Bernard Coleridge MP and Mr Henry Lopez were counsel for the prosecution, and Mr H.E. Duke appeared for the defence. According to a possibly very short-sighted reporter from the *Western Morning News*, the prisoner, dressed in a light tweed suit with white cravat, 'had a smart, healthy and intelligent appearance'. Such a description of a youth who had narrowly survived a suicide attempt and become grotesquely disfigured in the process hardly rings true. Though he had already confessed to his crime, committed out of jealousy, before the Tavistock police and magistrate, Williams pleaded not guilty in court, hoping to get a reduced sentence on the grounds of insanity.

The prosecution opened by stating that the prisoner had gone about his work at his father's mill with the revolver in his pocket for several days before the incident in November, and therefore had the deliberate intention of taking life. The statement he made to his father at the hospital was then read out. It concluded with Williams's description of how he threw himself in the river, found himself on a stone and called to the Lord for mercy, and ended with the hope that his parents would forgive him. In short, Coleridge said, there was 'great design, great determination, and continued forethought' prior to the murders.

Among the witnesses called were Emma's brother William and sister Elizabeth, who gave their version of the events of that horrific evening. Mark Bellamy, a farm servant, told the court that he had seen a man with his collar pulled over his head soon after the shots were fired and was sure it was 'Blucher' Williams, the nickname by which he was known by the other boys in the village, after the Prussian general at the battle of Waterloo whose name was a byword for boorishness. Superintendent Nicholls said that he had found the prisoner's coat in the River Tavy between Tavistock and Harford Bridge. In the pocket were a prayer book and a cartridge.

The defence made the best of the mental incapacity argument. Dr Broderick said he could not say in all honesty that there were symptoms consistent with the prisoner having suffered from epilepsy, but he had been given to believe that there was a history of insanity in the family. First and second cousins had been admitted to mental asylums. Dr Peter Dens, medical superintendent of Wonford Asylum, Exeter, had made enquiries as to the prisoner's background and had personally examined him, but concluded he was of sound mind and understanding. He saw no evidence of insanity.

Mr Williams, the prisoner's father, said that his son had always been delicate, and at seven or eight years of age he had had a severe illness of an epileptic nature. Since that time he had often complained of severe headaches. Earlier in 1892 he had an attack of influenza and never seemed quite the same afterwards. In the weeks preceding the murders, his behaviour was very strange. Two villagers in Peter Tavy testified to the latter. One said that Williams had a tendency to glare and look excited for no apparent reason, and another thought he looked half-dazed much of the time, as if he had just recovered from a fit.

'Murder must be the deliberate act of a man in the full possession of his senses,' the defence remarked in summing up, suggesting that Williams was not of sound mind at the time. The judge elaborated, saying, 'The law on this point was that a person to be excused for such a crime must be in a state of mind which rendered him not able to distinguish between right and wrong.' If the jury had reasonable doubt as to whether Williams was responsible for his actions, if he was acting under some sudden and uncontrollable impulse, he must be given the benefit of the doubt.

The jury took only twenty-two minutes to return a verdict of guilty, adding that they considered the defendant to have been perfectly sane when he committed the crimes. 'I trust the jury will forgive me', the judge addressed the prisoner, 'if I think that had they come to any other conclusion they would have been wanting in their duty. A more cruel and deliberate murder I have never heard of.' As Williams had planned the deed and purchased the revolver a few days earlier with that very purpose in mind, it was difficult to argue that he had merely acted on impulse.

While Williams was awaiting execution, a petition for his reprieve was organised by the Revd A. Harvie of Christ Church, Devonport. Harvie had obtained 12,522 signatories and the petition was presented to Queen Victoria, but the Secretary of State could find no grounds for reprieve. Williams probably never knew of the petition's existence. While in Exeter gaol he expressed some concern for the families of both his victims, and wrote long letters to his parents apologising for what he had done. In view of the circumstances of his deliberate cold-blooded double killing, it might not be too cynical to suggest that any belated penitence had a somewhat hollow ring. He found some consolation in reading the Bible and receiving religious instruction. On Thursday 23 March he was confirmed in the prison chapel.

On 27 March, the eve of his execution, he wrote a farewell letter to his parents, in which penitence and a startling certainty of going to heaven were equally apparent:

> You must not trouble about me, I shall be far happier. I shall soon be where no troubles come. . . . I am very comfortable under present circumstances. My time is very short, but it does not trouble me much. I feel how I deserve my punishment, and all I have been through seems like a dream. I have been for a walk this morning. It seems very beautiful to me, but heaven will be far brighter.

It was signed, 'From your loving son, WILLIE IN CHRIST. Goodbye.'

On the following morning crowds gathered outside the gaol. 'An air of depression seemed to come over many of those who were waiting to see the message of death hoisted on the black staff temporarily erected over the entrance,' the press noted. '"Will the bolt fail?" seemed to be the thought uppermost in everyone's mind, so deep was the impression made upon the public by the futile attempt in 1885 to execute Lee.' Memories of that notorious failure probably loomed large in the authorities' minds too, and no effort had been spared to ensure that the fiasco would not be repeated. At 8 a.m. the warder whose duty it was to hoist the flag over the parapet was seen to lift his hat, and this was accepted as confirmation that the procession was approaching the scaffold. Williams, it was said, 'displayed the greatest fortitude' as he walked with a firm step the few yards from the condemned cell to the scaffold. The hangman, James Billington, assisted by Thomas Scott, placed the rope around his neck, a burial service was read by the chaplain, and a white cap was pulled down over the prisoner's face. As the black flag was drawn into position, there was a sigh of relief among the crowds who then dispersed, 'satisfied that the executioner had done his work with promptness and despatch'.

Within six months another member of the families involved had died prematurely. Joseph Rowe had been shattered by his son's murder; his health rapidly deteriorated, and he was admitted to the Cottage Hospital at Tavistock where he died on 1 September at the early age of forty-seven. The official cause of death was a heart and lung complaint, but nobody doubted for a moment that a broken heart had hastened his end. He was laid to rest in the churchyard beside his son. His wife, Emma, was buried there on her death in 1912, and their daughter Alice in 1940.

The shock of the murders continued to reverberate around Peter Tavy for some time to come. Constable Callard, who had been involved in the investigation, was so distressed by the case that he had a nervous breakdown and moved away from the area a few months later.

# 21
# THE PARANOID PAINTER

*Devonport, 1900*

Frank Herbert Watts was a painter and decorator who lived at 64 Albert Road, Morice Town, Devonport. In 1900 he was aged thirty-six and his wife Mary Elizabeth (Bessie) was thirty-two. They had four children – Frank, aged eight, Lily, six, Charles, four, and Maud, sixteen months – with a fifth on the way. To others they gave the impression of being happily married 'quiet people, much respected' in the neighbourhood, though Frank's weakness was drink and its associated tendency to become quarrelsome after one too many.

On 6 July 1900 he went to work in the morning, but returned home earlier than usual, complaining of feeling unwell. Bessie advised him to go to the

*Albert Road, Morice Town, Devonport, c. 1900.*

doctor, and he promised he would in the afternoon. After a light lunch he told her he felt better, and then he went out, but did not return to work, coming home again at about 3 p.m. Around twenty minutes later their landlord, Cornelius Simmonds, from whom they had rented two basement rooms for several years, went out for a walk. He saw husband and wife before he left, noticed that Bessie was scrubbing the stairs, and had no reason to suppose anything was wrong – or, indeed, that anything was about to go wrong.

About two hours later he returned from his constitutional and heard loud groans coming from the basement. He knew Bessie was expecting another child and wondered if she had gone into premature labour. As he was elderly and not in the best of health himself, he was disinclined to go downstairs and see what was wrong. He asked his wife if she would go and find out, but she said she was nervous about doing so. The groans became louder and more prolonged, and then the children began screaming. Frank, the eldest, was at school, but the other three were at home. The family decided they would have to call the police and PC Edwards came to investigate.

What he found confirmed the Simmonds' worst fears. Bessie was lying, apparently lifeless, in a pool of blood on the basement floor, while her three younger children screamed hysterically. Just after PC Edwards arrived, Frank staggered in from the adjoining wash-house, his throat badly cut and bleeding profusely. He fell over his wife's body. It was noticed that he had a bloodstained razor in his hand. Edwards called Dr Kirton, who confirmed that Bessie was dead, her head almost severed from her body. Her husband had a 5-inch wound which had severed his windpipe, but no other veins appeared to be damaged. The doctor bandaged him and then took him to the Royal Albert Hospital, while the children were sent to the workhouse.

Two days later Frank recovered consciousness in the hospital. When he saw a policeman sitting by his bed, the memory of that macabre afternoon came back to him. He promptly sat up and tore the bandages from his throat in the hope of reopening his wounds and bleeding to death. He became so violent with the policeman, and a nurse who tried to restrain him, that it took the combined efforts of four or five of the more healthy patients to hold him down.

Once he had recovered he was taken into custody. He was charged with murder and attempting to commit suicide. On two separate occasions in the weeks leading up to his trial he was examined by Dr Dens from Wonford House Asylum. In the doctor's view, Frank Watts was quite sane, but suffered from delusions which were likely to recur. When they did, he would be dangerous and perfectly capable of committing a similar crime. Dens also found symptoms of epilepsy and alcoholism, and discovered that there was a history of insanity in Watts's family.

At the Exeter Assizes on 15 November, Mr McKellar and Mr J.A. Simon led the case for the prosecution, and Mr W.T. Lawrance for the defence. The prisoner pleaded not guilty to murder. During the trial he said that he was sure that other people were after him, hunting him, following him around in the hope of finding out something about him and hoping to take civil proceedings against him. His employer, Mr Trenerry, said that Watts had been 'strange' for some days before he killed his wife, a view which other residents in the house confirmed, testifying to Mary's complaints that her husband was behaving oddly and suffering from sleeplessness.

Mr Justice Ridley summed up at the conclusion of the evidence for the prosecution without any address being made by the counsel for the defence. He said that the only issue for the jury to decide was whether the prisoner was insane at the time he committed the act. Without retiring, they brought in a verdict of guilty of murder, but added that the prisoner was insane at the time. The judge said that Watts's conduct gave grounds for suspicion that he 'was not master of himself' and could therefore not be held responsible for his actions. A sentence of execution would be inappropriate, and he ordered the prisoner to be kept as a criminal lunatic in the gaol at Exeter for an indefinite period.

# 22
# ANGER ON THE FARM

In the summer of 1904 Hubert Baker, who owned and lived at Warcombe Farm, 2 miles from Kingsbridge, was a well-respected and generally liked man of twenty-eight. His widowed sister, Annie Cummings, to whom he had always been very attached, was his housekeeper. Baker was unmarried, and used to tell his friends that as long as Annie could look after him and help around the house, he could not wish for anything better. It was said that he had no enemies in the world, though unhappily there was one exception to the rule.

Albert Corner, a youth of twenty, was the fourth son of a tanner who lived at Goveton near Ledstone. He worked on the farm for Baker, though he was a far from ideal employee. Notorious for his surly manner and bad temper, he had already lost several jobs as a farmhand elsewhere because of his general laziness, insubordinate attitude and inability to get on with his fellow labourers. Baker was prepared to give him a chance, but frequently had reason to tell him off because of his attitude, threatening him with dismissal if he did not mend his ways.

After lunch on Friday 17 June 1904, Baker was shearing sheep, while Corner was leaning idly against a gate, watching. Baker reminded him that it was time he attended to the horses. Corner's response was to swear at him and pick up a crowbar, threatening he would come and flatten him. Having seen and heard similar threats before, Baker looked at him calmly and refused to react. After a moment Corner calmed down and dropped the weapon. Baker told Corner it was the last straw: he would have to go at the end of the month. He then went indoors to tell his sister, who was less patient than him with the young man whom she thought had had far too many chances already. She advised Baker not to put up with any more nonsense but to pay Corner off and have done with him at once. As in so many other matters, Baker decided that she was right. The next day Baker told Corner he was being dismissed, gave him the rest of his wages, and after tea Corner went to his room and packed his belongings, ready to go.

Baker then went out to take the cows into the field. Wilfred Perrott, the five-year-old son of Baker's neighbours, went with him. As they were crossing the field, Perrott looked in the direction of the hedge in horror, shouting,

*Ledstone Farm, near Kingsbridge, home of Edward Friend, who reported Baker's murder and Corner's suicide.*

'There's Albert with a gun!' Baker had had his back to the boy, and swung round to look where he was pointing.

Almost at once Corner, only a few yards away, fired at Baker and shot him in the face. Severely wounded, Baker fell to the ground but struggled to his feet, calling out in agony to his sister. He started to run down the hill, with Corner following him. The latter took aim again and hit Baker in the shoulder. He fell again, and soon afterwards died from his injuries. Perrott ran back to the farmhouse to fetch Cummings, who had heard the shots and was already on her way out. Two men were in the stables tending to the horses, and she asked them to come and help to find out what was going on. At first they thought there had been an accident. Then they caught sight of Corner, who shouted that he had 'killed the master'. Moments later there were two more shots.

One of the men had gone to fetch the police, and on his way he met Edward Friend, a horsebreaker from nearby Ledstone Farm. Friend was exercising his chestnut mare and he offered to go to the police station and report the incident. On their arrival, the police and the men from the stables found Corner in the field with the gun lying beside him. He had shot himself in the face, and death had been instantaneous. An area of flattened grass by the hedge suggested that he had lain in ambush for his employer.

When the news spread around Kingsbridge and the surrounding area there was the inevitable wave of morbid interest. According to the press, 'hundreds of people' walked out to the farm just to catch a glimpse of the scene of the tragedy, while the police did their best to restrain their curiosity and 'there were no unseemly incidents'.

At the inquest Wilfred Perrott was called on to testify, sitting on his father's knee in the witness box. He impressed everyone with the clear way in which he gave an account of the gory proceedings. In Corner's defence, his father said that his son had been subject to uncontrollable spasms and anti-social behaviour since being stung by a viper at the age of eleven. He also complained that the gun and cartridges should not have been left within such easy reach of his son, who was known to have an uncertain temper. As all farmhouses at that time had guns easily accessible for shooting rabbits for the pot, killing vermin and other sundry causes, this was not considered a valid complaint.

The coroner ruled that Albert Corner was guilty of wilful murder and then took his own life. As a murderer and a suicide, he was not entitled to a full funeral service and he was buried by lamplight at All Saints' Church, West Alvington, at 10 p.m. by the Revd T. Bell-Salter. A grave had been prepared at the head of the churchyard under a tree close to the hedge. This was considered unconsecrated ground and therefore appropriate as the resting place for a criminal. Corner's relatives refused to accept responsibility and it was left to the receiving officer, Mr Mundy, to make all the funeral and burial arrangements for the youth who had brought such disgrace on his family.

# 23
# DEATH OF AN ARTIST

## *Hatherleigh, 1905*

In the first years of the twentieth century Mary Breton, a spinster in her early thirties, was a regular visitor to Hatherleigh. Her uncle, Mr Isbell, lived at Claremont Villa in the town, and she stayed with him. She was an enthusiastic artist who enjoyed sketching and painting landscapes in the area, and she was well known to the locals as 'the artist'. They particularly appreciated her readiness to stop and chat to anyone, thus dispelling any impression they might have had that an artistic temperament went with a 'leave me alone' attitude.

On 15 May 1905, during one of her regular visits, Miss Breton found herself an attractive field near the River Lew. Cattle often used to come and drink from the water, and this must have provided her with the kind of picturesque view much loved by generations of rural painters. Before taking her materials she had told Mr Isbell that she would be home as usual in plenty of time for dinner.

As she was generally so punctual he became anxious when she failed to arrive. A friend joined him to go and search for her, and they went at once to the area where she had been working. The easel with its incomplete sketch was still by the river, and a few yards away lay Mary's body. Her head and face were badly disfigured and covered in blood. A doctor was summoned to confirm that she was dead.

Next day an inquest was held in the Court House at Hatherleigh in the presence of Mr J. Prockman, the Coroner for Dartmoor. It was suggested by one of those present that the deceased had been charged by a cow or bullock while sitting at her easel and the injuries were caused by the animal's horns. The jury returned a verdict that she died as a result of haemorrhage from head injuries, though there was nothing to show how these were caused.

At first nobody mentioned the word murder, and there the matter might have ended had it not been for the suspicions of Sergeant Hill, the police officer in charge at the town. He felt the verdict must be wrong, and that the presence of one man in the community might explain everything. John Ware had returned home about three weeks earlier from serving a sentence of twelve months at Exeter for indecent assault. Hill made enquiries and discovered that Ware was working at nearby Brimridge, ripping bark. He and

*Hatherleigh police station.*

other employees used to walk regularly along the Strawbridge footpath, through the area where Mary Breton had met her death. When questioned, other workmen reported that they had noticed her working at her easel during the previous few days.

When Hill found out that Ware had made an excuse to leave his workmates after work on the evening of Miss Breton's death at Lewer Bridge, close to one entrance to the Strawbridge path, he felt that the case was as good as solved. From further questioning around the town, he learned that Ware was lodging in the London Hotel and had returned there at about 8.30 on the evening of Miss Breton's death, over two hours after his workmates had last seen him. He had had a pint of beer, and seemed unusually nervous as he ordered it at the bar, his hands shaking and the legs of his trousers up to the knees soaking wet. Hill remembered that when the victim was found her skirt was wet – something to which no importance had been attached at the time of the inquest.

On 17 May Ware left his job and took up a new one at Hannaborough Quarry. Sergeant Hill went there to interview him, was dissatisfied with the answers he received, and asked him to accompany him to the police station for further enquiries. Once they were at the station, Hill sent a message to his nearest senior officer, Superintendent Bond at Holsworthy, asking him to come at once as he was fairly certain he had apprehended the murderer. Bond arrived half an hour later, and after the officers had discussed the case, they went to visit the scene of Mary Breton's death, leaving Ware secured in a police cell under the supervision of Constable Smith. Inspection of the area revealed marks on a grassy bank indicative of a struggle, and also several bloodstained stones.

Returning to the police station, they were met by a doctor and Smith. In a state of shock, the latter told them that Ware had been in his cell for nearly an hour, apparently quiet. When Smith went back to check, he found the prisoner lying on his back, bleeding profusely, with a scarf around his neck. They deduced that he had stood on the bed with the scarf acting as a tourniquet, preventing blood from reaching his head. When he became unconscious he fell onto the floor and struck his head. The doctor confirmed that the cause of death was strangulation.

On the next day a second inquest was held. This time there was no doubt about the verdict, namely that Ware had killed himself 'while of sound mind' in order to escape the punishment that he knew was coming to him. Nobody had any doubt, either, that he was the murderer of Mary Breton. Like Albert Corner a year earlier, he had committed suicide to evade the hangman. No one in the town was prepared to make a coffin for him, and he was buried on the edge of the local graveyard.

# 24

# AN UNSUITABLE YOUTH

Edmund Walter Elliott did not have a particularly promising start in life. He was born in about 1889 to an unmarried mother of sixteen, whose own mother had also been born outside wedlock. On two separate occasions Edmund's mother had been convicted for keeping a brothel at their home, 46 Well Street, Plymouth. In spite of this he did well at school, achieved good results in his examinations, and decided he wanted to enter the Royal Navy. This ambition did not last long, and soon after leaving school he was apprenticed to a hairdresser, Mr Atrill of King Street, at his mother's request. After completing his term or being dismissed, depending on whose version of events is to be believed, he was unemployed for some time, and planned to join the army.

As a small boy he had played from time to time with a group of youngsters in the district, one of whom was Clara Jane Hannaford, a girl three years younger than Edmund, who lived at 2 Henry Street with her parents, George, an artisan, and Fanny, and her four younger siblings. As the eldest child Clara was expected to help her mother around the house, and in this she proved herself to be a model daughter.

When Edmund was eighteen he became rather attached to her. Her parents never really approved of him or of their liaison, largely as they thought Edmund was an idler who seemed incapable of holding down a steady job. When they found out that he had probably fathered a child with another girl who lived in the next street, they decided he was a bad character and thought Clara could do much better for herself. In the spring of 1908 they told her they did not want her to see him again. She apparently agreed to break off the relationship, which had never been very strong. As she was still only fifteen, she was hardly old enough to have a serious boyfriend.

George and Fanny's dismay when they found out in the summer that Clara and Edmund had resumed their friendship can be imagined. That they started seeing each other again may have been anything but a voluntary decision on Clara's part, as the family thought she was afraid of Edmund and felt it would be unwise to do anything that might provoke him to violence against her. After her parents had prohibited her from seeing him again, he frequently threatened to 'do for her'.

An incident in July 1908, the month Clara celebrated her sixteenth birthday, suggested that this was not necessarily an idle threat. One night he climbed in through her bedroom window to where she was sleeping in the same bed as her younger adopted sister, Elsie Gill. Edmund woke her and said he had come 'with the full determination of doing for you with a knife'. Although she must have been more scared than amused, she told him not to be so silly because he would wake Elsie. 'Very well,' he retorted, 'if she screams I will do the same to her.' At this point he evidently thought better of it and went away again.

When Fanny Hannaford heard that Elliott had broken into her daughters' room and threatened them, she vowed to give him a piece of her mind. She came round to his house looking for him, and when he came out to see her she hit him in the face and knocked him down. A policeman had to be called to separate them.

At this time Clara's uncle was serving in the Royal Navy aboard HMS *Leviathan*. He became friends with another young seaman, William Johnstone Lilley, who lived six doors down from Elliott in Well Street, and took him back to the house at Henry Street to introduce him to the family. They took an immediate liking to him, and George and Fanny probably thought that he would be far better company for their eldest daughter than the ne'er-do-well of Well Street. On the evening of 17 November Lilley was ashore, and he asked Clara if she would accompany him to the Palace Theatre of Varieties. She said she would prefer the show at the Theatre Royal, to which he agreed. When he came to the house early that evening to collect her, he arranged to meet her parents at the Athenaeum Hotel after the show, and they left the house at about 7.30 p.m.

They left the Theatre Royal after the performance finished about three hours later. As they were walking back to the hotel, Elliott approached Clara in the street and whispered something to her. She spoke to him for a few minutes, and Lilley clearly heard his last words to her – 'If you come up the lane, I'll prove it.' Clara and Lilley went into the hotel, where they met her parents and he bought himself a glass of ale. She told him she was going home to take her hat off, which struck him as a rather odd excuse for leaving, but she assured him she would be back in a few minutes.

There were at least two witnesses to what happened next. At about 10.45 John Tremlett, a labourer, heard a scream, and saw Elliott with his arm locked around Clara's throat. He followed a trace of blood which led to the rear of 25 Queen Lane. Another person in the area, Mary Seccombe, whose husband Fred was a professional boxer, had known the Hannaford family for some years. She recognised them, and heard Elliott say, 'I want to speak to you a minute, Clara.' 'I will come down if you won't touch me,' she replied.

*The Theatre Royal, Plymouth, behind Derry's Clock, 1907. Clara Hannaford and William Lilley saw a show at the theatre on the evening she was murdered, 17 November 1908. The theatre was demolished in 1937 and the present Theatre Royal, which occupies a nearby site next to the clock, was opened in 1982.*

Mary then watched in horror as they walked together, before he violently attacked Clara and knocked her hat off. She ran after them, picked Clara's hat up and made sure that the girl was not seriously hurt. She then handed the hat to her and asked Elliott what he thought he was doing. 'It is nothing to do with you,' he answered brusquely. She told him that she would tell the Hannafords what he had done.

True to her word, a few minutes after leaving the hotel, Clara returned. She was staggering, and a gaping wound in her throat bled profusely. She tried to speak to her mother, but her injuries were so severe that no words came out. Lilley bound a handkerchief round her throat in an effort to stop the flow of blood and covered her with his coat, while he and Fanny got ready to take her to the Homoeopathic Hospital at Lockyer Street. Two officers, Sergeant Beer and Police Constable Quantick, were on duty outside in George Street, and they phoned the station for an ambulance.

People had realised that something unpleasant was going on, and a large crowd was gathering to see exactly what was happening. Had they not tried to satisfy their curiosity, the poor girl might have been saved, as the policemen had to spend several minutes keeping them back and getting through to the victim. It was to no avail, for Clara collapsed and died from loss of blood before they could get to the hospital. Her body was taken to the mortuary at Vauxhall Street, where it was seen that the larynx was cut right across and the wound on her throat went from ear to ear.

After the crowds had dispersed, Mr Tremlett followed the trail of blood to Queen Lane and the spot where Clara had been attacked. Searching with the aid of lighted matches, outside one of the doors to a back entrance in the lane he found a large quantity of blood and near it a heavily stained razor, which he picked up carefully and took to the police station.

Having had his revenge, the murderer went back to his home at Well Street, changed his bloodstained coat and then walked to the Central Police Station where he arrived at about 11.30 p.m. and asked Inspector Hitchcock if they were looking for 'Ted Elliott'. He was arrested on a charge of murder, warned and cautioned, to which his reaction was, 'Is she dead?' On being told that she was, he confessed that he had cut her throat with a razor. 'She has been out with another young man tonight,' he added. 'I met her and did it, and put her to rights.' When questioned further, he said the crime had not been premeditated, but done on the spur of the moment. He was searched and formally charged with wilful and malicious murder.

A friend of Edmund's family went to tell the news to his mother and stepfather, a dock labourer, who had only been married since August 1907. They said that he generally seemed quiet but happy at home, especially as he had just finished his hairdressing apprenticeship satisfactorily. The stepfather was aware that he had quarrelled with Miss Hannaford, but was amazed that he should have resorted to such violence. The police later came and searched the house, and found Elliott's bloodstained coat. As for the Hannaford family, when she was told her daughter was dead, Fanny broke down and wept, then said she must go to the scene of the tragedy. One of Clara's sisters and her grandmother, both weeping bitterly, went straight to the hospital to ask if she really was dead, unable to believe that such a dreadful thing had happened.

Over the next two or three days the scene at Queen Lane became a magnet for sightseers. So many people came to look that a number of constables had to be placed on special duty. Though all tell-tale signs of the gory event had been cleared up, public curiosity was slow to diminish.

An inquest was held at Vauxhall Street on 19 November. Such was the public interest in the tragedy that an hour before proceedings were due to open, a large crowd consisting mainly of women and children had gathered outside the premises. Once again police had to be summoned to keep everyone under control. The main witnesses drove to the mortuary in a cab, which was immediately surrounded. If onlookers had come for a sight of the murderer himself, they were disappointed, for Elliott was given the opportunity of attending but chose not to, and was instead represented by John Ickle from solicitors Bicke & Wilcocks. The foreman asked why the accused was not present, as he certainly ought to be there. The coroner said he had been in touch with the prison governor, who told him that Elliott could have come if he wanted to, but 'I think he is just as well out of it'. Among those who had come to the inquest were George Hannaford, the victim's father, William Lilley, Mary Seccombe, John Tremlett, Dr Parsloe, Sergeant Beer and Inspector Hitchcock, who had prepared a detailed plan of the streets and lanes surrounding the scene of the attack. The jury took only two minutes to consider their verdict, and unanimously decided that it was wilful murder. At the same time, they also passed a vote of condolence to the parents of the victim.

That evening Clara's body was placed in a coffin and taken to her parents' house. Her funeral took place at the Plymouth Cemetery, Ford Park, on the morning of Sunday 22 November.

Elliott went on trial at Exeter Assizes on 11 March 1909. His case was heard by Mr Justice Ridley, with John O'Connor and Raymond Asquith as counsel for the prosecution, and Mr W.T. Lawrance for the defence. When called to the witness box, Fanny Hannaford said that she had known Elliott for nearly two years. Though he had been a barber's assistant part of the time, she had the impression that he would not work and that he was 'of bad character', citing his illegitimate child in the next street as proof. When the defence asked her about the courtship between her daughter and the prisoner, she denied that their relationship was ever anything more than a brief friendship, as her daughter was only fourteen when they first knew each other. Pressed to admit that such an age was a little young for her daughter to

# PLYMOUTH TRAGEDY.

## STRUGGLE IN THE LANE SEEN BY A WOMAN.

## ACCUSED'S THREATS.

## VERDICT OF "WILFUL MURDER" AGAINST ELLIOTT.

The inquest on Clara Jane Hannaford, the victim of the tragedy in Queen-lane, Plymouth, on Tuesday night, was held in the Mortuary, Vauxhall-street, last evening by Mr. R. B. Johns, borough coroner. Quite an hour before the time for the opening of the inquiry a huge crowd had gathered. The number became so great that a special force of police had difficulty in controlling the traffic. The great majority of the crowd consisted of women and children. The principal witnesses drove to the Mortuary in a cab, which was at once surrounded. No doubt the large number of persons had assembled in the expectancy of seeing the accused, Edmund Walter Elliott, but in that they were disappointed. Elliott was given the opportunity of attending, but he preferred not to do so. Mr. John W. Bickle (Bickle and Wilcocks) represented him. Mr. Southern was chosen foreman of the jury.

### PLAN OF THE SCENE.

The Coroner remarked that Inspector Hitchcock, of the Plymouth Police, had prepared a plan of the streets and lanes in the district in which the terrible affair occurred, and no doubt it would greatly assist the jury in their investigations.

### CORONER'S STATEMENT.

The Coroner, addressing the jury, said they were not often called together to consider a case of this kind in Plymouth. The facts, however, were simple. It appeared that a girl not quite sixteen years of age apparently kept company with a young man named Edmund Walter Elliott for some time, and he (the prisoner) was informed the parents objected to this. There was a young man named Lilley, an able seaman of the Royal Navy, who served in the same ship as the deceased's uncle, and from that source he became introduced to the girl's family. From a suggestion which Lilley made to Clara Hannaford, they were to the Theatre Royal on Tuesday evening, and it was understood with the parents' consent. It was also arranged that after the performance they should meet the girl's parents in the Athenæum Hotel, and this they did. Whilst Lilley and deceased were passing down Athenæum-lane from the theatre a young man, said to be Elliott, whispered something to her, and was also alleged to have said: "If you come down the lane I will prove it." After going into the Athenæum Hotel and seeing her parents the girl ap... parently l f...

*Detail from the* Western Morning News, *20 November 1908, reporting the murder of Clara Hannaford.*

*Ford Park Cemetery, Plymouth.* (© Hannah Lindsey-Clark)

be going out with a boyfriend, she asserted indignantly that they never went out, and 'it was only girl and boy play'.

While there was never any doubt as to the outcome, Mr Lawrance suggested that in view of the lack of forethought, it might have been more accurate for them to call the crime manslaughter rather than murder. Much was made of the prisoner's bad start in life and his mother's character: 'A more squalid and a more unhappy condition than the birth of this young fellow could not possibly be imagined.'

Moreover, as a child Elliott had often suffered from fits and there was a history of insanity in the family – his great-grandmother had died in a lunatic asylum seven years previously. His mother, Mrs Emma Bryce, said that he had been subject to fits until he was five and a half years old. On the day before Clara's death he had been very unwell with pains in his head and all over his body, and on the day itself he had stayed in bed until about 6 p.m. She added that he had always been most industrious when not unwell. He had only lost his job as a hairdresser because of pains in his head and shaking, which made customers reluctant to be shaved by him.

In summing up for the prosecution, O'Connor said that the prisoner's mind was full of malice. He was consumed with jealousy because the deceased was going out with another young man, and he had waylaid her with the intention of taking her life. As he was carrying a razor at the time and had had it in his pocket the whole evening, and as he had already once threatened to kill her, this was a crime nothing short of wilful and malicious murder.

In conclusion, the judge called it a lamentable case, especially in view of the prisoner's family background. Nevertheless, there was another, more serious consideration – the nature of the crime itself. Edmund Elliott had clearly intended to kill the deceased, and the jury had to make up their own minds as to whether he was insane. If not, he was responsible for his actions.

The jury delivered their verdict of guilty after just fifteen minutes. As Elliott was only nineteen years old, they made a recommendation for mercy on account of his youth, but it had no effect. Passing sentence of death, Mr Justice Ridley told Elliott he should not place any hope in being reprieved. Standing in the dock, the prisoner seemed totally unmoved. He was hanged by John Ellis and William Willis on 30 March, the first murderer to die on the gallows at Exeter in the twentieth century.

Broken-hearted George Hannaford did not survive his eldest daughter for long. He died on 21 December 1910 at the early age of forty-seven. At the time of his death, his address was given as 3 Trafalgar Place. Fanny lived for nearly thirty years after the tragedy, dying on 23 January 1938 aged seventy-one. Both were laid to rest in the same grave as Clara at Ford Park Cemetery.

# 25

# THE WORK-SHY
# EX-SAILOR

## Plymouth, 1912

George Cunliffe, who was born and brought up in Wigan, joined the Royal Navy as a young man. He was discharged in 1912 at the age of twenty-seven after five years' service, though he remained part of the Special Reserve. Moving to Plymouth, he met Kate Butler, a woman two years his junior. She was separated from her husband, who had been in the Army Service Corps but was now a hawker at Chatham. They moved into a house together, but their happiness was short-lived. In common with many other men of his age who had left or been discharged from the services, Cunliffe was restless, could not or would not find proper work, drank too much and had a reputation for being quarrelsome. Not surprisingly, their relationship soon deteriorated.

Butler regularly gave him small sums of money, and on 2 November handed him a sovereign which he immediately spent on drink and gambling. That night he threatened her with a chair, and said he would 'do' for her and her sister, Cordelia Graham, who lived nearby. The police were called and he was arrested for being drunk and disorderly. At the Stonehouse police station, PC Easterbrook was asked, 'Do you know Kitty Butler?' He said yes, only to have Cunliffe tell him drunkenly that he would 'do for her'. He would have been released on payment of a fine, but Kitty was determined to teach him a lesson and refused to give him any more money. As a result he was sent to prison for five days. While serving his sentence, he complained bitterly to one of his guards about the treatment he had received at the hands of the woman with whom he lived. The guard thought he might be intent on revenge once he got out, but managed to calm him down. Cunliffe then said that on his release from prison he would probably return to Wigan.

On 8 November he was a free man – but not for long. Returning home that morning he found Mary Hocking, the wife of a blacksmith who had been a fellow-resident in the house. She told him that Kate had moved, and he asked if he could come into the house to shave as he had left his razor behind, a request she readily granted. Once he had found the new address, 72 King Street, he went to see Kate and found her lying on the bed reading a newspaper. Sitting in the same room was her friend Susan Gill. Having just come out of prison, a sentence which he would probably not have served if only Kate had paid the necessary, Cunliffe was still very angry. Taking a chair by the window, he ignored her at first. He lit a cigarette, and Susan gave him a glass of porter. At length he turned to Kate. 'I want my fare to Wigan,' he told her brusquely. 'I have not got it,' she answered. 'You had better go to the docks, get a boat, and get away out of it. You can't stop here.'

Susan went out of the room to fetch something, and when she returned Kate was on her hands and knees looking for some footwear. Suddenly Cunliffe, incandescent with rage, seized her by the throat and put his hands round her neck. She screamed for Susan to fetch the police. When Susan had gone, George locked the door, took a razor and slashed Kate's throat. As PC John Pearce arrived, Cunliffe told him he had 'done her in', said he wanted them to die together, and then tried to cut his own throat as well. Kate lay bleeding profusely, but was still just conscious and asked faintly for something to drink. She was so badly injured that she died about half an hour after the attack. When Dr Vawdrey reached the house, just too late to see the woman alive, he said her wounds were so terrible that he would never have been able to save her. The fatal cut, 17 inches long, almost encircled her neck.

Cunliffe's self-inflicted injuries were critical and he was taken to the Homoeopathic Hospital where he remained for several days. An inquest was opened on 26 November but adjourned because he was too ill to attend, and the coroner reported, rather surprisingly, that Cunliffe was 'in such a state at the present time that he is not aware of the woman's death'.

The trial was delayed for several weeks until he had fully recovered. The case was heard at Exeter Assizes on 3 February by Lord Justice Coleridge. Mr Emanuel and Mr MacDonald led the case for the prosecution and Mr Scobell Armstrong for the defence. Cunliffe pleaded not guilty, but the prosecution said there could be no question of self-defence as he was not insane. The defence argued that if the crime was not committed in a drunken frenzy, then it must have been the act of a madman. The victim's wounds were so severe that they could not have been inflicted by anybody but an insane person.

It took the jury six minutes to reach a verdict of guilty. When the prisoner was asked if he had anything to say about why the judgment of death should not be passed upon him, he said, 'I didn't know why I did this. My mind must have been unhinged.' As the judge sentenced him, he stood in the dock apparently unmoved. He made no effort to appeal and was hanged at the gaol by John Ellis and George Brown on 25 February 1913.

# 26

# THE THWARTED NAVAL STOKER

James Honeyands, a Londoner, was a naval stoker of twenty when he first met Amanda Bradfield shortly before Christmas 1912. She had come to Plymouth to see her husband, who was serving on board HMS *Monmouth*, which was about to go for service on the China station. As Honeyands had no relatives in the Plymouth area, Bradfield allowed him to lodge at weekends with her and her mother, Edith Jane Perry, at their house in Stonehouse Lane. He became very fond of eighteen-year-old Mrs Bradfield, and she behaved with perfect propriety, refusing to look on him as anything other than a lodger and a friend. This was not good enough for him, and on one occasion during the summer of 1913 he told her that he hoped her husband would be drowned before he landed in Plymouth again. 'If you don't have me, I'll watch that you don't have anyone else; I would rather shoot you.' Shortly afterwards he left the house, perhaps as a result of being asked to go.

Absence inevitably made the heart grow fonder, or the spirit more determined. He would not take no for an answer. In August he was drunk when he called at the house. He asked Mrs Perry where Amanda Bradfield was, made some verbal threats, and produced a revolver before being persuaded to leave the premises. This was not the last time that he was seen or heard in the area vowing revenge on the young woman who would not abandon her husband for him. On 4 October he talked about Mrs Bradfield with an acquaintance, John Davey, saying that he 'nearly did for her once; it is a pity I didn't do for her right out'. Unusually, he appeared stone cold sober at the time.

It was a different matter two weeks later. Honeyands had heard that Mr Bradfield was due to return home on leave, and all his old jealousies came to the surface. On the evening of Saturday 18 October Amanda was enjoying a drink at her local, the Courtenay Arms at the junction of Courtenay Street and Union Street. Honeyands suddenly walked in, caught sight of her and began to argue with her, saying, 'You will be all right before the night is out if I get my hands on you.' A youth overheard him, slipped out and went to tell Mrs Perry that he suspected her daughter was being threatened again.

At length Honeyands gave up, or appeared to tire of the argument, and stormed out, somewhat the worse for drink.

When Mrs Bradfield followed him out of the pub not long afterwards, the argument started again in the street. Matters became progressively more heated and he made an impertinent suggestion, to which she retorted, 'My husband is a gentleman, not a cur.' 'I'm no cur!' he snapped back, as he took a revolver out of his pocket and fired three times in Amanda's direction. One bullet missed but the other two went through her. As she fell on the pavement, seriously wounded, he tried to shoot himself, but the revolver failed to fire. The noise had brought some of the bar staff and customers on to the street, and they were in time to see at least one shot being fired at Mrs Bradfield. Mrs Perry fainted, but was otherwise unharmed.

Honeyands now tried to run off, but Albert Harvey, a postal worker who had been standing nearby, heard the shouts of 'Murder, stop that sailor!' He gave chase and Honeyands pointed the weapon at him, then against his own temple, but still it would not fire. Harvey threw him to the ground and wrenched the gun out of his hand. Several more men in hot pursuit helped to hold him down until PC Southern arrived and took him to the police station.

By now barely conscious, Mrs Bradfield was rushed to the Homoeopathic Hospital, but her condition gradually worsened. In a fit of coughing she brought up one of the bullets, but the damage was already done and she died of her injuries on the evening of 28 October, the immediate cause of death being the breakdown of the right lung caused by a bullet wound.

Honeyands was charged with murder and committed for trial at Exeter on 3 February 1914. (By coincidence, it was exactly a year to the day since Cunliffe had entered the same dock.) As proceedings were about to begin and members of the jury were being sworn in, one juror objected to his participation because he did not believe in capital punishment. He was promptly excused from service.

For the prosecution, Mr R.E. Dummett told the court that the prisoner had been of exemplary character, and it was with regret that the story he had to unfold was 'a most squalid and tragic one, in which drink, vice, jealousy, and revenge played parts about which, unhappily, they were too accustomed to hear in these courts'. Several other men who worked at the docks were aware of the defendant's fearsome reputation, and testified to the fact that when drunk he was 'fair mad'. Two other stokers confirmed that he had been in this kind of state on the night of the tragedy; one, Thomas Craven, admitted that 'if he had a little extra drink it made him fighting mad'.

The counsel for the defence used the regular mitigating circumstance that there was insanity in the family. From the police station at Plymouth, Detective Inspector Hitchcock had made extensive inquiries as to any evidence of unsound mind among Honeyands's relations. He found out that his paternal grandmother had been in Coney Hatch asylum for thirty years and that his mother died in a 'drunkards' home' following at least one suicide attempt. The prisoner himself had never exhibited any evidence of derangement during his early years. He had been a model pupil at the East London Industrial School from 1904 to 1907, and before joining the navy had gone to work on a farm in Wales.

In summing up, Mr Commissioner Harrison said that the prisoner was accustomed to dealing with firearms, and that he had definitely meant to kill Mrs Bradfield. He added that 'it would be a most disastrous state of the law if a man who had taken some liquor which might inflame his passions to some extent could turn round and say he was drunk when he committed the crime'. It took the jury ten minutes to find him guilty, but they added a recommendation to mercy. This was dismissed, and Honeyands was hanged by John Ellis and William Willis on 12 March 1914.

# 27

# THE SOLDIER AND THE SCHOOLGIRL

## *Plymouth, 1916*

Few murders incite such revulsion as the killing of a child, and fortunately there have been few of this nature in Devon. One, the last in the county to result in execution, occurred during the First World War.

Late one night in December 1915 there was a knock on the door of the Gregorys' house in Alexandra Road, Plymouth. A soldier, Frederick Brooks, explained that he was a private in the Worcestershire Regiment. He had just been in the area to attend a funeral, but had been delayed, missed his bus and was unable to get back to his camp at Tregantle. He would be very grateful if they could provide him with a bed for the night. Arthur, a ticket collector by profession, and his wife, Clara, were happy to oblige.

Twice the following year Brooks, who was aged twenty-eight, from Tipton in Staffordshire, and married with one child, came to call again, once in March and once in June. On both occasions the Gregorys allowed him to stay overnight and have breakfast with them before he left. But Arthur Gregory thought there was something peculiar about the man, and after he had gone the second time, he told Clara that he did not want her to take Brooks in any more.

Four days after this third and final visit, on Tuesday 20 June, Brooks was in Plymouth once more. This time he went to the school in Alexandra Road which Alice, the twelve-year-old daughter of his hosts, and her younger sister used to attend. Arriving soon after 11 a.m., he told the headteacher that his name was Private John Jones. Why he resorted to this alias was never explained, but he said he had been given a message by Mrs Gregory that Alice had her permission to leave school to run an errand for her and take him to a shop near the adjoining area of Mutley Plain. Alice Peek, the girl's schoolmistress, spoke to her in order to confirm that she and the family knew Brooks, and a few minutes later he and Alice left the school. They were seen walking together towards Compton at about 11.30.

When Alice's sister left school a little later she returned to the house alone. Thoroughly concerned, Mr Gregory went to look for his daughter in the grounds near the school, then reported her missing to the police station at Bedford Street. Next he searched the parks, Plymouth Hoe and the pier, returning to the police station at about 5.30 p.m. By this time the grim truth was out.

About an hour earlier Brooks had also gone to the police, found an officer, Constable Wyatt, and told him that he wanted to give himself up as he had just killed a young girl. 'I don't know what made me do it,' he said. 'I must have been mad or in a fit of temper for a minute or two. She was dead when I left her – I strangled her.' Wyatt arrested Brooks and he offered to show the officer everything. 'If you put a pair of cuffs on me I will take you where she is in the field.' Wyatt, PC Pearce and Detective Westlake took Brooks in a taxi to Efford Lane. Here, at a field between the lane and Lower Compton, the prisoner pointed over the hedge and said that Miss Gregory was in the lower corner.

Wyatt stayed with Brooks while the other two searched for Alice's body. They discovered her 18 feet from the hedge, with her arms by her side and her hat over her face. Her neck and face were discoloured, and she had been dead for several hours. All around her the grass was trodden down over an area about 12 feet by 6 feet, indicating that she had put up a struggle. Her clothes had not been disarranged, which suggested that there had been no sexual assault. The officers called Dr Sedley Wolferstan who arrived at about 6 p.m. to see the body and said that the girl had been dead for five or six hours. He confirmed that death was due to asphyxia. There were small abrasions on the windpipe and chin, and general bruising.

Although it was so often used by defence counsel as a mitigating circumstance, in this case there was a strong possibility that Brooks might have been mentally unbalanced. On 3 November he went on trial at Exeter Assizes, with Mr Radcliffe Cousins leading the case for the prosecution and Mr F.J. Tucker for the defence. The prosecution said that the victim had only been twelve and a half years of age, but looked at least two years older, and was 'comely', thus implying that the prisoner might have had the intention of violating her.

Brooks pleaded insanity and his brother Joseph from West Bromwich, the only witness for the defence, gave evidence that he suffered from fits, severe depression and 'attacks of morbidity', during which he would frequently break out 'into attacks of unexplained violence'. In extreme cases he might throw bricks through shop windows or threaten violence towards the family, and on recovering he would have no memory of what he had done. He had had frequent fits during his childhood, though once he reached the age of seven they became less regular. This enabled the counsel for the defence to claim that the crime had been committed in a moment of temporary insanity. As Brooks had freely confessed to killing Alice Gregory, the only question that remained was whether he was responsible for his actions.

Any tendency to mental abnormality might have been exacerbated by Brooks's wartime experiences and the effect that serving in the army during the war had on soldiers of a sensitive nature. Nevertheless, the jury were not convinced and only took thirty-five minutes to return a verdict of guilty. The counsel complained that Mr Justice Rowlatt had not properly put the case for the defence to the jury and lodged an appeal, which was dismissed.

Brooks went to the gallows on 12 December. Like Honeyands, he was hanged by John Ellis and William Willis.

# 28

# THE KILLING OF SISTER CATHERINE

### *Torquay, 1916*

Annie and Catherine Barton were two spinster sisters who lived together at Kirkthorpe, a small villa in Rousdown Road, Chelston, Torquay. In 1916 Catherine was aged forty-nine, Annie fifty-one. For three years Annie had been subject to attacks of mental illness which increasingly led to physical violence against her sister, and one nurse after another had to be brought in to look after her. With care and medical treatment she seemed to be recovering, and in June the nurses were discharged. A lady's companion was engaged in

*Chelston, Torquay.* (© James Cosgrave)

their place, though a nurse used to come in occasionally just to check that everything was in order. Before Annie's problems, the sisters had slept together, and now Catherine decided that it was safe enough for them to resume this practice.

Six weeks later, tragedy struck. At about 6.30 a.m. on 7 August the Bartons' servant, Ethel Maclaren, heard loud knocking coming from the bedroom. She went to see what was the matter and tried to open the door, but a call from inside of 'It's all right, I can manage', which she thought was Annie's voice, went some way to reassure her for a moment. She went back to her work, but the noises resumed a little later. Increasingly worried, she called for the next-door neighbour, Charles Bartlam, who arrived at about 7 a.m. As the noise was getting louder, he forced the bedroom door open. He and Miss Maclaren found Catherine lying at the foot of the bed with her skull battered in and blood spattered around the room. A heavy stick with a large knob on the end was lying on the floor and it told them all they needed to know. Still wearing her nightdress, Annie was leaning over her sister when they forced their entry, but as soon as they came in she stood up.

Bartlam went back to his house and told his wife what he had found. A doctor and a

policeman were summoned. Dr Himely confirmed that Catherine was dead, then PC Tucker arrested Annie. When she was dressed, he took her to the police station at Torquay. Later that morning she was brought up at the police court before the chairman, Mr J. Taylor, and charged with wilful murder. Throughout the hearing she looked down at the floor, apparently in a semi-dazed condition. She spoke only when she was asked to confirm her name.

As far as everyone knew, there had never been any quarrelling between the sisters, and Annie must have committed the killing in a moment of frenzy. An inquest at Cockington Parish Rooms the next day came to the same conclusion.

Nevertheless, she was committed for trial at Exeter Assizes on 3 November, the same date as Frederick Brooks. She pleaded not guilty. During the proceedings, it emerged that Catherine had been anxious to hide any knowledge of her sister's condition and had actively resisted all efforts and attempts to put her in an asylum. The stick with which she had been battered to death was in their bedroom as a precaution in case of burglars. Nurse Cannon, who had helped to look after Annie, said that she had attempted several acts of violence against Catherine. Annie, the nurse told them, was under the delusion that Catherine had sinned gravely and it was her duty to kill her. Mr Bartlam said that he thought the accused did not seem to realise what she had done. She looked at him and then at Catherine's body in a strange way, asking herself all the time what she could do to atone for her sins.

Mr Justice Rowlatt suggested that there was nothing to be gained by proceeding with any further evidence. It was obvious that Annie Barton was 'a raving lunatic' when she committed the crime. He directed the jury to pass the only verdict possible – guilty but insane. This they accordingly did and she was sentenced to be detained at His Majesty's pleasure.

# 29

# THE FATAL ATTRACTION OF TWO COUSINS

*Plymouth, 1920*

At the age of twenty-one, Cyril Victor Tennyson Saunders was a lance-corporal in the Royal Engineers, stationed at Crowborough in Surrey. For the previous two years he had been going out with his cousin, Dorothy Mary Saunders. Aged sixteen, she was also from an army family, born in India, where her father had served with the Royal Fusiliers. After he retired from the forces, the family returned to England, settling in Southampton. Dorothy's parents died within a few months of each other, and in June 1920 she came to Plymouth to live with another cousin, Mrs Elizabeth Lawrence. The latter had a tobacconist and confectionery shop at Percy Terrace in the Lipson Vale area of the town, and Dorothy regularly worked behind the counter. Cyril was falling deeply in love with her, and decided that he wanted them to become husband and wife.

Until now, Cyril had shown every sign of becoming a promising soldier. He had been briefly on active service in Russia, and was well liked and respected by everyone. His senior officers found him cheerful, good tempered and one of the smartest NCOs in his unit. Off the parade ground he had several interests, and particularly enjoyed singing, sports and reading.

Everything started to go wrong on 24 July 1920 when he was accidentally struck on the head with the butt of a rifle while on guard duty. Had it been a direct blow, the doctors thought, he would probably have been killed, or at least left with severe brain damage. As a result of the injury he was in hospital for about ten days, and on his discharge he was very changed in his manner. He 'flared up' at the smallest thing, often stared around with a vacant expression and was startled by sudden noises. On one occasion he and Lance-Corporal Tilford heard a dog howling at the camp. Saunders grabbed Tilford's arm in horror, 'For Christ's sake, what was that?' Tilford had to reassure him that it did not necessarily signify impending death. When he was giving evidence at a military court against the man who had hit him with the rifle, he was very nervous, fumbled with his hands, and seemed quite different in his demeanour from the normal self-confident soul of a few weeks previously.

Worse was to come. Early in September, while he was on leave, Cyril came to Plymouth to visit Dorothy. Whether they were officially engaged by now is open to doubt. He had certainly set his heart on marrying her, and she may have agreed to do so, later telling him that she wanted to break it off. On the other hand, she might have denied ever having agreed to become his wife, and sometime after that told him that she never promised him anything more than friendship. He suspected that while he was in Surrey she was seeing somebody else, something she fervently denied.

Though she was reluctant to admit it at first, Dorothy had discovered to her horror that she was probably carrying Cyril's child. Convinced that he had been supplanted in her affections, a furious Cyril asked for 'his' name, saying that he did not intend to hurt the boy, but (rather contradicting himself) he would surely kill anybody else who dared to come between them. When Dorothy remained adamant that it was all over between them, Cyril returned to Surrey after his leave was over. He hoped that the rejection of his affections had been an isolated aberration on her part, and he intended to get her to change her mind.

If this was his hope, he was doomed to bitter disappointment. A few days later Dorothy wrote to reiterate that she did not wish to marry him. He replied on 14 September:

> I warn you, if I do not hear tomorrow, I shall be in Plymouth on Thursday, and although I hope it will not be necessary yet, possibly, there will also be trouble coming for someone. Perhaps it is unfortunate, but I happen to love you a good deal more than you may think, and remembering your promises, I don't intend to stand anyone fooling around and helping you to break them.

He followed this letter with another three days later, in which he addressed her by her pet-name of Bubbles:

> You need not be afraid that I will make trouble if you tell me his name. This is the second time I have stopped myself from fulfilling my vow; but, Bubbles, as surely as any other fellow ever attempts to come between us again, I shall murder him in cold blood with my own hands. All the pleadings, tears, or explanations will not save him. That is my oath, which I swear on the Bible before me now. Bubbles, my precious, write soon, my beloved, for my heart is breaking, with the torture of this last two days. Answer my questions and make your promises again, for your old boy has forgiven you, darling. G.B.Y. [God be with you], and help you to keep true and loving to me. My darling, I am more unhappy

today that I think I have ever been in my life before. It seems all my world is crumbling around me. All my heart's deepest love and devotion, and my most tender kisses, dearest love of my heart.

Ever your own true and devoted boy, Cyril

She answered on 20 September, making it clear that as far as she was concerned, it was all over between them:

Dearest Cyril, It's no good, Cyril, I must tell you. I know I'll just about break your heart, but I don't feel at all now as though I could get married. You have spoilt all my trust in you, dear. Don't think, Cyril, there is any other boy, for there isn't. My heart will always be turning to you, but it's no good when you have lost all trust in me. If it is God's will that I should have a baby I'll let you know,* but I must bear the brunt myself. Don't do anything rash, Cyril, look after yourself, and please answer this.

Yours, Bubbles

On receipt of this letter Cyril sent her a telegram warning her of his imminent return, and he was back on the train to Plymouth within a few hours. He took a taxi from North Road station straight to Mrs Lawrence's house, and begged Dorothy to reconsider. She refused, telling him it was no use his coming to see her as she was 'still of the same mind'. Mrs Lawrence left them talking in the kitchen while she went to serve in the shop. In the course of conversation Cyril became desperate, and threatened to go and put his head on the railway line. At this, an unnerved Dorothy called Mrs Lawrence back to talk some sense into him. As Mrs Lawrence came into the kitchen, Cyril walked out but she followed him, caught him up, and told him firmly not to do anything silly as there was not only himself and Bubbles to consider. How would his parents feel if he killed himself? Having talked him out of it, she invited him back to the house for a cup of tea, and he accepted. While they were drinking she admonished him: 'Buck up and be a man! In a couple of months you will think of what a fool you've been!' At this he burst into tears.

While Dorothy said she did not want to be friends with him any longer, she agreed that she would go to the cinema with him that night. They came back at about 10 p.m., and after their return Dorothy complained to Mrs Lawrence how tiresome he had been throughout the evening. Nevertheless, he was allowed to stay at the house that night, and as he said goodnight

* This letter is reproduced from the *Western Morning News*. Its sister daily, the *Western Evening Herald*, also published it, but instead of the words 'I'll let you know' quotes the text as 'I will (marry?) you'.

to his cousins, he told them he would turn the gas on. Mrs Lawrence was so uneasy about this that she went downstairs and turned the gas off at the mains. Dorothy then told him not to do anything silly that night, assuring him she would think it over and give him an answer in the morning.

Next day, 23 September, at about 9.30 a.m. she took him a cup of tea. Half an hour later he came downstairs and had breakfast, during which he read a newspaper, saying barely a word to the others. At 11 a.m. he went out, returning a couple of hours later. He had tried to buy a revolver, but was unable to do so. Instead he purchased a hunting knife for 8s 6d, telling the vendor that he was about to go abroad. He then went into a public house and had a couple of drinks.

What happened next was described by Mrs Lawrence to a newspaper reporter that afternoon:

> They were quite friendly last night, and [Dorothy] told him that though she did not intend to marry him she would treat him just like the rest of the boys. He stayed here last night, and this morning went for a walk alone, returning for dinner about one o'clock. Dorothy was not here when he returned, as she had gone for a walk through the fields to keep out of his way. He promised me faithfully and on his oath that if she came back he would not lay a finger on her, and that neither would he do anything to himself, so I went out to find her and we returned to the shop together.

As long as she would let him see Bubbles once more, he said, he would go straight back to the camp afterwards, and promised he would not even write to her again.

All three went into the kitchen, and Dorothy asked Cyril if he was really going back to the camp. 'Yes,' he answered, 'by the 2.50 train, if you give me dinner.' At that stage a customer entered the shop and was attended to by Dorothy, followed by Cyril. He stayed in the shop until the customer was served and had left, and then there was a quiet conversation between them both which Mrs Lawrence could not hear. It continued for some time until a piercing cry of 'Betty! Betty!' startled the house.

Mrs Lawrence heard a scuffle, and on looking into the shop she saw Dorothy with her hands up to her throat. At first glance it looked as if Cyril was strangling her. Dorothy screamed again, and Mrs Lawrence saw blood coming from her mouth. She ran into the shop, shouting frantically, 'You brute! Don't touch her!' Cyril then laid Dorothy on the floor. Mrs Lawrence saw the bloodstained knife in his hand. She snatched up the scoop and scales from the counter and hurled them at his face, then ran into the street screaming 'Murder!' From the street she saw Cyril standing in the doorway of the shop, calmly smoking a cigarette. After a few minutes he turned as if to walk away and she shouted, 'Stop that man!' 'Did you think I was going to run away?' he asked her. When she said she thought he was, he said he never intended to, and went back into the shop.

Meanwhile, another soldier, James Boote, was sitting by an upstairs window in one of the houses opposite. At the sound of muffled screams he jumped up to see what was happening, saw Dorothy lying across the doorway of the shop, immediately telephoned for an ambulance, and then ran across the road. Cyril was still standing there, looking quite unconcerned. 'There is no use your doing anything,' he said calmly, 'because I have done her in; I have stabbed her through the heart.' A crowd was beginning to collect round the doorway, so Boote persuaded Cyril to come back to his house until the police arrived. As they crossed the road, Cyril told him, 'I have courted her for two years and she chucked me up.' When the police came he handed them the knife. 'You may as well have this,' he suggested, aware of what lay in store for him. 'I am not going to kill myself. Someone else will do it for me.'

PC Quantick was the first to arrive, and he formally arrested Cyril. When Deputy Chief Constable Martin charged him with murder and cautioned him, Cyril said, 'I have nothing to say. I had a couple of drinks this morning, and by telling you that it may help me a little.' When he was searched, a handkerchief stained with blood and an undated letter signed 'Bubbles' were found in his coat. He made a full statement to PC Dawe, starting with the morning's events and his going into town. At the time, he said, he was wearing Dorothy's watch and she was wearing his. When he returned to Percy Terrace he was told that she had gone out, so he waited for her, 'and when in the doorway of the shop we were in the act of changing watches, I took out the knife and stabbed her with it. She fell down. I placed the knife on the counter and one man who I do not know came in and took it away.'

Lipson Vale was normally one of the quieter residential areas of Plymouth, but the tragedy, reported the local press, turned it into 'the scene of much subdued excitement'. Several people were attracted to the vicinity of the shop, all gossiping about the crime. As the family was well known, several callers came to bring Mrs Lawrence their heartfelt sympathy in person.

On 9 November Cyril went for trial at Exeter Assizes, pleading not guilty to murder before Lord Justice Coleridge. Counsel for the prosecution were Mr Holman Gregory and Mr Edward Duke; for the defence were Mr W.T. Lawrance and Mr J.L. Pratt. Among the witnesses to be called were Mrs Lawrence, Private Boote and Dr Wolferstan, who confirmed that the injuries to the deceased would have caused her death within a few minutes.

Two other witnesses gave evidence suggesting that the prisoner was slightly abnormal. Sergeant McGregor of the Signal Corps gave him a good character reference, but after the incident in July when he was struck on the head, McGregor saw him wandering around the camp at Crowborough 'with a faraway look in his eye, and I reported the matter'. Dr H.G. Pinker, medical officer at Plymouth gaol, said he examined the accused on his arrival. He considered him mentally normal and he remained thus all the time he was in his charge. On cross-examination, he said that a blow on the head 'might occasion cerebral mischief if the skull was injured. Following severe concussion mischief might occur periodically at times of excitement.'

Opening the case for the defence, Mr Lawrance said that it was impossible to contradict the facts of the tragedy. He intended to call evidence to show that the blow on the head had materially altered the accused's state of mind. Lance-Corporal Tilford and other colleagues from Crowborough all testified to the change for the worse in his demeanour.

Throughout most of the proceedings Cyril maintained his composure, but he had to work hard to control his emotions when his father, Mr T.B. Saunders of Camberley, told the court that after the blow, his son became irritable and listless. Dr Alfred Turner, who maintained a private lunatic asylum at Plympton and had had many years' experience in mental cases, had examined the prisoner and considered that such an injury might produce insanity. The unhappy and tragic love affair through which he had just passed, he added, might predispose him to mental trouble, especially at his age. All that had been said pointed to the fact that the blow on the head, coupled with the affair, led the prisoner to become unbalanced and irresponsible. Such an insane state of mind might not be continuous, and it was possible the prisoner would become fairly sane after the murder. When cross-examined, he said that a superficial head wound would not be enough in itself to cause insanity.

Addressing the jury, Mr Lawrance said that they had to consider in what degree the accused was responsible for his actions. Did he know exactly what he was doing, and if so, did he know that he was doing wrong? Conceding it was difficult to establish insanity in a direct way, he told them it would be best to return a verdict of guilty but insane if there were any doubt. The prosecution, he averred, was possibly at fault in suggesting the murder was caused by a desire for revenge and prompted by jealousy, as the material change in the prisoner's mental condition after July was undoubtedly aggravated by the shock he received in Dorothy's letter on 20 September.

Summing up for the prosecution, Mr Holman Gregory said that the law dealt with insanity from a point of view different from the way in which it would be approached by a doctor in charge of a lunatic asylum. When the accused bought his knife, he had no doubt as to what he was going to do with it. There was no doubt that he was madly in love, desperately jealous, and in the eyes of the law he knew that he was going to kill his cousin. He had weighed the consequences, whatever they might be; he knew that he was doing wrong, and there was only one possible verdict.

Summing up, Lord Justice Coleridge said there was merely one issue in the case, that of the responsibility of the accused for the act of which he was

*Percy Terrace, Plymouth, 2006, little altered since 1920 when Dorothy May Saunders was murdered at her aunt's shop.* (© John Stapley)

undoubtedly guilty. When he committed the act, did he know that it was contrary to the law? If he did, he was responsible; if he did not, then he was not. If he knew he was doing what was contrary to the law, then he was guilty in the eyes of the law. If the jury were of the other opinion, then their verdict would be one of guilty, but that the accused was insane at the time. He further directed that such a verdict was not to be returned merely on the grounds of sympathy or compassion.

After retiring for ten minutes the jury returned a verdict of guilty, the foreman adding that they were unanimous in their verdict of wilful murder.

'No one who has heard this case will doubt that the attempt to prove you were mentally insane has failed,' the judge remarked before passing the death sentence.

You knew well the difference between right and wrong, for the murder was premeditated. No sudden gust of passion carried you away. You bought the weapon wherewith to kill your victim. You determined that if she was not to be yours she should belong to no one else. With four determined strokes you slit the thread of a bright young life. Truly it has been said that jealousy is as cruel as the grave. The law is not vengeance; it is punishment with justice. There is one retribution that you can effect, and the way is by remorse, by sorrow, and I trust, by penitence.

Cyril Saunders received the verdict without flinching, though he was seen to shrug his shoulders as he was escorted away. While in custody he left a letter thanking the prison officers for the kindness they had shown him during his time in the condemned cell. He went to the scaffold on 30 November. The executioners once again were John Ellis and William Willis.

# 30

# SHOOTING ON THE MOOR

## *Whiddon Down, 1927*

Richard Lane and his sister Emma, who was the elder by twelve years, were brought up in the village of Winkleigh in West Devon. As a young man Richard moved to London, where he kept a draper's shop in Lambeth for some years. By about 1911 he had made a reasonable sum, and decided to give up the business. In 1925 he moved into a boarding house in Lambeth Palace Road, but he was careless with his money. By July 1927, when he was aged fifty-six, he had come to the end of his financial resources, being £120 in arrears for board and lodging. He told the landlord he was going to Devon to see his sister and borrow enough from her to pay off his debts. He said he would take his rent book with him to show her how much he owed. For the previous seven weeks Emma had been staying at Thorn Farm, South Tawton, a village on the north-western edge of Dartmoor about 8 miles from Okehampton, as she had done regularly over the years. The farm was owned by Arthur and Mary Knapman, who had known the Lanes since they were children. Richard arrived on 15 July and seemed in his usual good health.

On the afternoon of Wednesday 20 July they all joined in the haymaking. Richard was preparing to move house and settle down with Emma, intending they should go back to London. She wanted them to stay in Devon and choose a house near Torquay.

Sometime during the day she gave her brother two £100 notes. At about 7.30 that evening they went for a walk towards Whiddon Down, a stretch of moorland about 250 yards from the main Exeter to Okehampton Road to check on the times of morning buses to Exeter, from where they were planning to take a train for London the next day. Mary Knapman's son offered Richard a gun as he had talked of shooting a couple of rabbits for their supper.

Emma, who was aged sixty-eight, suffered increasingly from rheumatism and did not like to stay out late. When they had not returned by 10.30, Arthur Knapman started to become worried. He and his son went to the neighbouring farm, Torrhill, owned by their friend Thomas Branton, in order to help organise a search party. Taking a lantern each, they checked over the

*Dartmoor.* (Courtesy of Ted Gosling)

nearby fields. After finding nothing they returned to Thorn Farm, found one of the labourers, Mr Cousins, and asked him if he had heard any firing in the vicinity. His sister told them she had heard a shot just before 10 p.m.

The search party resumed their task, and at about 2.15 the following morning they discovered the bodies of Richard and Emma in the bracken in Pitts Head Field, between the farm and Whiddon Down. Emma was dead and Richard was unconscious. They had gunshot wounds in the side of the head, and a double-barrelled shotgun lay between them. Both barrels had been discharged, and a bootlace was attached to the trigger of the right barrel. No trace was found of any other person who might have been in the vicinity.

Taking Mr Knapman's son with him, Mr Branton got into his car and went to Okehampton to find a doctor and a policeman. He returned a little later with Dr Hughes and PC Brewer. Richard was driven to the town's cottage hospital with injuries from which he was not expected to recover. Emma's body was taken to farm buildings at Wells in preparation for the post-mortem and then her funeral on the following Monday, 25 July, at Providence United Chapel, Throwleigh.

*Whiddon Down.* (© Paul Rendell)

An inquest was held on 23 July. The Deputy Coroner, Mr G.J. Atkinson, asked everyone present to keep an open mind on the case. 'The time for considering the verdict, if it comes at all, will come later. In the circumstances, it would not be proper, or possible, or just to form an opinion without giving Mr Lane an opportunity of hearing the evidence and, if he so desires, of making a statement.' The doctor said it would be several weeks before Mr Lane was likely to be in a fit state to testify, and the inquest was adjourned.

When Richard Lane came round, PC Hutchings from Okehampton visited him at his hospital bed. Though still very weak, Lane seemed determined to catch up with his attackers – of whose existence he professed to be certain. 'I want to get up,' he told the policeman.

> You and I want to catch them – the men who did this. There are two of them. They shot me first – bang, then my sister. I saw her lying there after they had killed her. It was the money they were after. She had it on her, about £8,000. She always carried it about in a bag under her clothes.

*Providence United Chapel, Throwleigh.* (© Paul Rendell)

It was my money, I gave her all I had when I was being pressed by –
[solicitors]. She was just going to let me have some to pay my debts in
London with, when it happened. They took it all and left in a car. Now I
have got nothing. We shall have to go to London; that is where we shall
find them. I do not know them, and should not recognise them again.

Nobody believed that any other party was responsible for the attack. Lane
was charged with murdering his sister, and sent for trial at Exeter Assizes on
1 November. He pleaded not guilty to murder. In court he said that during his
career as a draper in London he had made about £10,000, but after deciding
to retire from business he withdrew the entire proceeds – a small fortune in
those days – from his account in cash and handed it all to his sister. He was
visiting her in order to get money to pay his bills when the tragedy occurred.
They were out walking in the field that evening when she handed him £100 in
notes, and then he saw two men jumping out from beside the hedge. They
struck him with something, and he had no recollection of anything else until
he recovered consciousness in hospital. When questioned about having
handed her £8,000, he said he had given her £50 'in big Bank of England
notes' when she came to London.

For the prosecution, Mr Hawke said that when the bodies were found there
was no sign of a struggle involving anybody else. In view of Richard Lane's
debts, he must have come to the end of his tether, and had probably killed his
sister in sudden anger because she would not give him any money.

For the defence, Dr R.N. Craig, an expert in nervous diseases with a
practice in Torquay, and Dr Richard Eager, superintendent of the Devon
Mental Hospital, Exminster, agreed that the prisoner was insane, and had
probably been in such a state at the time of the killing. Craig said that when
he saw Lane in prison, he found his conversation disconnected and rambling,
his behaviour being that of 'oscillation'. He seemed to be suffering from
severe depression, and was possibly in the early stages of senile dementia.
Eager said that the prisoner's case had been complicated by the head injury,
which would have produced or exacerbated any behavioural problems that
they had discovered.

There was no apparent reason for why he should have deliberately killed his
sister. Three witnesses – Richard's former landlord from Lambeth, Stanislaus
Bowell, Mary Knapman and William Marshall, a retired draper from Exeter
who had known the Lanes for over forty years – told the court that he had
never spoken of her in anything other than the most affectionate terms, and
that they had always been very close. Had there been some ill-feeling between
brother and sister which nobody else had seen? If so, a sudden flash of temper
and the availability of a shotgun had proved a lethal combination.

Concluding for the defence, Mr W.E. Batt outlined the details of the
prisoner's business career, and his return to Devon with about £10,000. Later

Lane realised the whole of his property and handed the cash to his sister, who carried it around her waist. When he required any she would give him a small amount. Mr Batt asked PC Brewer if it was possible that Emma might have shot Richard and then herself, but Brewer said the position of the bodies when they were discovered ruled that out.

In his summary, Mr Justice Shearman said he hoped that the law would always be that 'a man was not found insane simply because he brought a doctor forward to say so'. The jury took twenty minutes to find Lane guilty but insane, and he was ordered to be detained during His Majesty's pleasure. This, said the judge, was 'a very proper verdict'.

# 31

# THE BODY IN THE ALLOTMENT

*Exeter, 1927*

James Livermore, a jobbing gardener aged about sixty, lived at Morgan Buildings, south Wonford, Exeter. He sold produce from several allotments, and was a familiar figure at local country and farming sales. Everywhere he went, he carried a large sum of money in a small tin or bag. Sometime during recent years he had received £53 in compensation after an accident, and chose to keep the money with him rather than deposit it safely in a bank or savings account. As has already been seen, he was not the first trusting soul in Devon whose reluctance to be parted bodily from a significant amount of cash was to prove his death sentence.

By the summer of 1927 he was living in the same house as his daughter and a distant relative by marriage, Reginald Morey, aged twenty-four, who was also a gardener by profession. On Sunday 26 June 1927 Morey told Livermore that he knew a woman who wanted to buy some rhubarb, and they made arrangements to fetch some from an allotment at Salter's Road, Wonford. In the afternoon Livermore told his daughter he was going there, but planned to return soon afterwards. A little later his son-in-law called round to see him, and waited for some time. He was increasingly worried when there was no sign of Livermore by early evening.

He went to the allotment and to his horror found Livermore's dead body concealed under some sacks and matting. He promptly contacted the police and sent for a doctor, who took the body to the mortuary at Exeter. Livermore had died as the result of a deep wound on the side of his back under the neck, which had penetrated the spine.

At about 8.45 on the Tuesday morning, Detective Sergeant Russell saw Morey wandering around in a field at Waterford Lane, and asked him to come to the police station to assist with enquiries into the case. Morey made no attempt to deny what he had done, and made a full statement of what had happened on that Sunday afternoon. After luring Livermore to the allotment on a false pretext, he waited until the older man was stooping with his back to him to cut the rhubarb. He then took a humane killer, which he had stolen from kennels at Paignton where he had previously worked, shot him, took his money out of the velvet bag, then hid the empty bag and the body. Morey had owed a certain amount to the landlady at his previous lodgings, and the first thing he did after leaving the scene of the crime was to pay her off. The next day he went to Exmouth where he bought himself some new clothes. As a result of his statement, he was remanded in custody for a week.

After being committed for trial, Morey appeared at Exeter Assizes on 2 November before Mr Justice Shearman and pleaded not guilty to murder. For the defence, Mr W.E. Batt said the prisoner was insane and therefore not responsible for his actions. His sister, Violet Morey, who lived in Paignton, said in evidence that she had often seen him lying across the bed, pulling horrible faces. He had had a severe attack of influenza in February 1926, after which he became potentially violent and his mother, unable to cope with him any longer, asked him to get lodgings elsewhere. Others who knew him said they had sometimes heard him screaming and shouting in bed at night. All this, said Mr Batt, seemed to suggest that he was probably certifiable under the Mental Deficiency Act and therefore not responsible for his actions. On the other hand, Dr Neville Craig, a specialist in nervous diseases at Exeter and Torquay, had examined Morey in prison. He said the defendant was not certifiably insane, and that he knew right from wrong.

When asked if he had anything to say, Morey told the court, 'I was told to do it. It is the voices. For days before I did it they said to me, "You must kill him."' Though the general opinion was that he had the mental development of a child of about twelve, it took the jury only seven minutes to find him guilty of murder. The judge passed sentence of death, adding at the same time that he would send reports of the doctors' evidence regarding Morey's mental condition to the Home Secretary.

Morey's execution was due to take place on 22 November, but a few days before the allotted date he was reprieved on the grounds of insanity and his sentence was commuted to penal servitude for life.

# 32

# MASSACRE AT WEST CHARLETON

*West Charleton, 1936*

Most of the murders described in this book were relatively straightforward cases in which the culprits were swiftly apprehended and brought to justice. One of the most horrific, a triple killing, failed to lead to any conviction. What happened one summer evening at Croft Farm, in the small village of West Charleton, near Kingsbridge, will never be known for certain.

Thomas Maye, a 71-year-old farmer, his seventy-year-old wife Emily and their daughters (Emily) Joan, twenty-eight, and Gwyneth Florence, twenty-five, had lived there for some time, and the family had farmed at Croft for several generations. Mrs Maye was active in church affairs and the Mothers' Union, while the daughters had been Girl Guides and were members of the Kingsbridge Hockey Club. Joan was also a teacher at the local Sunday school. They seemed to be a normal, happy, churchgoing family, well liked in the area, comfortably off and apparently with no enemies. Two other children were married. Mary lived with her husband at Aveton Gifford a few miles away, and Jack, a civil engineer, lived in India with his wife and two children. Thomas, his wife and daughters were frequently seen in West Charleton and around the area, and everyone considered the farmer very active and healthy for his age.

Also living in the house was Charles Lockhart, the Mayes' general servant and gardener. Aged twenty-two, he was one of five orphaned children from a Modbury family whose father had been killed in an accident at the mill where he worked. He had been with the Mayes for three years, and had his own bedroom at the back of the house.

On the evening of 11 June 1936, Lockhart was going out to a dance at Stokenham. He went off duty at 7 p.m. After leaving the house, he returned briefly at about 9.30 p.m. to collect an overcoat, letting himself into the outer kitchen through the back door and going up the back stairs to his room. While he was there he heard voices in the dining-room, which he assumed were those of Mrs Maye and her daughters. He also noticed that two men, Mr Maye's accountant Victor Smith from East Allington and a farrier,

William Stear from Aveton Gifford, had called at the farm to discuss routine business.

At 2.45 the following morning Lockhart came back to a house of horror. As he opened the door he could hear feeble groaning, and he saw a stream of blood seeping into the kitchen under the closed door from the adjoining upper kitchen. Gwyneth was lying on the floor downstairs between the hall and the kitchen, bleeding profusely from severe injuries to her head and a deep cut in her shoulder. Her pet spaniel was licking her face. Beside her was a cushion or pillow which it was thought she may have used to shield herself from her attacker. Without stopping to investigate further, Lockhart went to fetch the village policeman, Constable William Mugridge. Frank Lee, another of the farm labourers, was still around, and he came back with them to help.

They found the house reeking of paraffin, with some of the furniture and beds ablaze. Fuel had been poured on the stairs as well as in the bedrooms, but Mugridge was able to put part of the fire out by himself. The carpet and window curtains in some of the rooms were still ablaze, and Lee and a couple of others set to work with buckets. They formed a chain of water carriers until the flames were under control. If Lockhart had not returned when he did, they all realised later with a shudder, the entire house might have been gutted.

Joan was lying dead upstairs in the passage outside her bedroom, her skull fractured. In her parents' room Thomas was lying semi-conscious on a burning bed with a deep cut on his forehead and injuries to his jaw. When Mugridge entered the room, Thomas asked, 'What are you doing? Where has my wife gone?' On the floor beside the bed was the partly burnt body of Emily, who had also died of a fractured skull.

Mugridge then committed two cardinal errors. First, he failed to caution Maye before he spoke, and second, he uttered words that, if they were not tantamount to an accusation, came uncomfortably close. When Maye asked the policeman what he was doing in his bedroom, Mugridge replied, 'Your wife has sent for me as the house is on fire.' Maye asked him next where all the blood was coming from, adding that his head was very sore. Mugridge said he had sent for the doctor, and then asked 'What have you done?' As time would show, the question was easily misconstrued.

A walling hammer (a hammer and an axe combined), minus part of its shaft, was found lying beside Gwyneth. The missing part of the shaft was later found next to Joan's body. Lockhart had been using it in the garden the previous day, and put it in a china cupboard in the kitchen. He had meant to return it to one of the outbuildings, but was distracted at the time by the need to look for some other tools. There were pools of blood in rooms both upstairs and down, and particularly on Joan's bed, where it was assumed she had sustained most of her injuries before staggering out to the passage to die. The immediate assumption was that Mrs Maye was the first to be attacked,

*Kingsbridge Cottage Hospital, which was opened in Duncombe Street in 1898.* (Courtesy of the Cookworthy Museum)

and that her daughters had done their best to protect her, but ultimately met with the same fate.

At 4 a.m. Dr Robinson arrived, and first he examined Gwyneth. The smell of paraffin from her head and the coats that had been put over her to keep her warm was overpowering. He had her rushed to Kingsbridge Cottage Hospital, but the matron, Miss Duffy, took one look at her and guessed from the extent of her injuries that she did not have long to live. Her face, legs and shoulder were very badly bruised, and she died at about 8.30 a.m. without regaining consciousness.

Maye was told by the doctor that he would be taken to hospital as well but he refused, saying that the men would be coming for milking and he was expecting a delivery of manure. He was well enough to get out of bed and dress unaided. When Robinson looked at Maye's injuries, he found three cuts on his head, under each of which there was a fracture to the skull. Such wounds, he said, could only have been caused by someone striking the farmer with the walling hammer which had killed the rest of his family, and they were sufficiently severe to precipitate immediate unconsciousness. Though initially Maye seemed well and determined enough to carry on about his business as normal, his loss of blood, his age and above all the fact that he was suffering from severe shock, had to be taken into consideration. Robinson told him he needed a complete rest, and he would require a prolonged period of convalescence.

When more police arrived at dawn, they searched the property and were convinced that there had been no intruder. Three out of four of the family were dead, and there was blood over much of the house, with several imprints of bare, bloodstained feet. Maye was questioned by Inspector West. He was very frank and open, giving complete details of what had happened earlier the previous evening, even down to what the family had eaten for supper. He mentioned that the girls had been out to watch some night filming at Blackpool Sands, had had a long day, were extremely tired and wanted an early night. When he was asked what occurred later on, he said, 'I can't tell you. I wish I could.'

That morning Maye was moved to Kingsbridge Infirmary. Dr Robinson found that he was still answering questions lucidly, but could give no explanation for his injuries. When questioned, he had a clear recollection of events of the Thursday evening up to 9.30 p.m. His last memory was of what turned out to be the final farewell to his wife. He was going upstairs to bed and they passed on the stairs as she was coming down. She put her arm around him and gave him a kiss and a punch in the ribs as she told him she had some mending to do but would come up and join him shortly. 'That was the last time I saw her,' he added poignantly.

Though he had been able to dress unaided and read his watch at 5.20 at the farm that morning, his condition had deteriorated in the last few hours. As a result of haemorrhaging and swollen eyelids, now he could not even open his eyes. In the afternoon he was moved to a nursing home at Plymouth, where he spent the next few weeks under treatment. He regularly asked for his wife and daughters, as if unable to accept that they were dead.

As the only other surviving member of the family in the area, it fell to Thomas's daughter, Mary Wroth, to shoulder the sad burden of making arrangements for the triple funeral. Though the Maye family grave was some miles away at Staverton, near Totnes, on this occasion it was deemed appropriate for the service and burials to take place at St Mary's Church, West Charleton, on 16 June. Charles Lockhart was among the mourners, and eighteen farm workers from the neighbourhood acted as bearers. The three coffins, each surmounted by wreaths of roses and carnations, were laid in the chancel, while a psalm and the hymn 'Rock of Ages', a favourite of the family, were sung by the congregation. As Emily Maye and her daughters were interred in a single grave in the churchyard, within sight of Croft Farm, a guard of police officers was still clearly visible around the latter. The graves were lined with flowers by members of the Hockey Club, where Joan and Gwyneth had made so many friends.

On 15 July Maye was informed that he would be indicted on a charge of triple murder. He protested his innocence: 'I think it absurd making that accusation as I loved my wife and daughters too well.' At first a degree of suspicion also fell on Charles Lockhart, the only other person who was

*The Maye family grave at St Mary's Church, West Charleton. The facing panel shows a dedication to Emily and Thomas; panels on the other side are inscribed with the names and dates of death of their daughters, Joan and Gwyneth. (© Kim Van der Kiste)*

known to have entered the house during those hours. However, there was no reason to doubt his presence at the dance at Stokenham on the Thursday evening, especially as others had vouched for him.

Two weeks later Maye was formally charged at Kingsbridge Police Court. A model of a skull was displayed on the table for demonstration purposes; other exhibits included the walling hammer with broken shaft, bundles of clothing and stained carpet, and five bloodstained flagstones.

For the prosecution, Mr G. Roberts (who was later to become a judge himself) said that the prisoner was a man of exemplary character, and as far as everyone knew, he had always led a perfectly happy domestic life. After the murders, there was no sign of 'burglarious entry, and there was no sign of any robbery, although there was money, jewellery, and other articles of value in the house'. No motive could be suggested, no credible reason why he should have turned on his family, and his previous record rendered such crimes 'almost inconceivable on his part'. All Mr Roberts could suggest was that some trick of the mind, some temporary mental derangement, had suddenly changed a devoted husband and father into 'a homicidal maniac whose actions were controlled, not by reason, but by some murderous instinct'. It was perfectly clear, he went on, that Maye had not received his injuries in bed and remained there after being assaulted. His nightshirt was dirty with soot and charring, his feet were caked, bloodstained and dirty, and the dirt smelled of paraffin and blood, as if he had been walking for some considerable distance in such conditions. The filthy state of his hands seemed to confirm the same.

For the defence, Dr Robinson confirmed that Maye would have become unconscious almost immediately after being attacked. When counsel for the defence, Mr Laskey, asked if the injuries were consistent with the blows having been struck while the accused was in a lying position, the doctor said that they appeared thus to him, and it seemed impossible that any person could inflict such injuries on himself. When asked to suggest who had committed the murders, Maye was at a loss to say anything.

Further evidence was given at a second hearing the next day. Constable Mugridge reported that the spaniel belonging to Gwyneth smelled strongly of paraffin. One of the labourers brought back to the scene of the crime on the night, William Lamble, said that the constable left him to keep an eye on Maye's bedroom while he went to get help, and handed him a truncheon with the words, 'If he comes for you, knock him down.' Leonard Bevan, Master of Kingsbridge Public Assistance Institution, assured everyone that when Maye was brought there, his hands were covered with a substance which looked like lamp black and smelled of paraffin.

When asked for his own version of what had happened, the prisoner said that he and his family before him had lived at Croft Farm since 1840. He was on the best of terms with his wife and daughters, and as far as he knew he did not have an enemy in the world. He could not recall any conversation with police officers, and the first he knew of the fate of his family was when he learned from the solicitors of their deaths: 'I told the matron of the hospital that I knew something must be wrong, as my wife would be the first to come if she knew I was bad.' When asked if he had any financial worries, he said he did not. He had never seen the walling hammer, and declared that it did not belong to him. Pressed as to how his hands and feet could have become so dirty, or how blood came to be in various rooms, or who set fire to them, he could not explain. His mind was still a complete blank from 9.30 on the evening of 11 June, when he went to bed, until he found himself in a Plymouth nursing home.

Counsel for the defence, Mr F.S. Laskey, submitted that there was no case to answer. He asked the magistrates to believe the medical evidence that Maye had received his injuries while lying in bed, and that there was no considerable amount of blood anywhere in the house but on the bed itself. If Maye had been struck such severe blows while in the bed, they could not possibly be self-inflicted and he was surely not guilty of the charges of killing his wife and daughters. Nevertheless, after an adjournment of about fifteen minutes Mr Ashley Froude, Chairman of the Magistrates, announced that the bench had decided that the case should be submitted to a higher court.

On 9 November Maye, dressed in grey overcoat and black tie, still bearing scars on his face and forehead, appeared at Devon Assizes before Mr Justice Charles on three charges of murder. As the trial opened, Mr Roberts said that it would be part of the case for the prosecution that the individual who murdered Emily Maye also murdered her two daughters. The prosecution had no wish to press for a conviction, and did not intend to persuade the jury to find the prisoner guilty. Their sole duty and desire was to place the facts before the court. Mr Roberts's words seemed to anticipate the final outcome of the proceedings. He emphasised that 'the hand of the burglar or thief was entirely absent, and there was no sign of any entrance from outside', thus implying that the prisoner was the only person who could have perpetrated the crime.

Among witnesses called by the defence were accountant Victor Smith and farrier William Stear, who had visited Maye soon after 7 p.m. on the evening of 11 June. They agreed that everything at Croft Farm appeared perfectly normal. 'Do you know [Maye] as a kindly dispositioned old gentleman?' asked the judge. 'Yes, ever since I have known him,' was Stear's reply. 'Was he on affectionate terms with the family?' 'Yes.' A less affectionate portrait emerged from the testimony of others, who said that Maye was quick-tempered and mean with money. Walter Farr, a wheelwright who had worked for him for thirty years, told the court that he had been increasingly shaky and irritable of late. After a recent argument Maye had walked away, muttering angrily, 'If I were a younger man I should feel like hitting you.'

Constable Mugridge's question to the prisoner of 'What have you done?' at the scene of the attack, it was suggested, was out of order. 'Without any evidence whatsoever,' said Laskey, 'you made up your mind that my injured client was guilty of murdering his wife and daughters.' Roberts said he was sure the judge would realise the position with which the officer was faced.

When questioned about the medical evidence, Dr Robinson said that the bruises on Maye's jaw were consistent with his having been struck while under the bedclothes. 'Do you think it conceivable that he could have done it to himself?' asked the judge. 'Not the least bit,' Robinson replied. The judge said that he would feel bound to put to the jury that it was more likely, upon the evidence, that the prisoner had been attacked by someone else than that he had attacked his wife and daughters. Concluding the case for the prosecution, Mr Roberts said he would call no further evidence.

At the direction of the judge, the jury returned a verdict that Maye was not guilty of murdering his wife. He was then formally charged with murdering his daughters, and on each count the jury found him not guilty.

In summing up, Mr Justice Charles said that for the first time in the whole of his experience, the jury had been told at the opening of a murder trial that the case had only been lodged after the Chief Constable of the county and the Director of Public Prosecutions had most carefully considered the matter. 'Having made this a public matter in the opening to the jury, I feel bound to say that I think, after close consideration of the doctor's evidence, that the man might have been spared this ordeal.' He added that he wanted it to be understood that he was not attacking the prosecution, 'who appeared to have called every witness who could have been of any assistance to the defence, including the vital witness, Dr Robinson. If they had not called him, he could not have stopped the case, but the Crown, with that fairness with which it always acts, called the witness and put all the evidence before you to consider. I think we need discuss it no further.'

Maye looked dazed at the judge's words. When he had recovered from the shock, he waved a hand to somebody in court and was assisted from the dock. He left by a side entrance to be met by a couple of friends outside who congratulated him, and by his son, who led him to a car and swiftly drove him away. Later he spoke briefly to the press. 'Thank God that terrible time is over,' he said. 'I knew I would be proved innocent.'

As the case for the prosecution had been demolished so quickly, nobody had any chance to put forward possible alternative theories in court. A few years later, Roberts said that it was possible Gwyneth and her father might have had a struggle on the stairs for some unknown reason, and maybe she fell, thus receiving the injuries from which she died the following day. As she alone had had time to put on a dressing-gown and slippers, she was not attacked while still in bed. The hammer bore traces of hairs belonging to both of Gwyneth's parents and her sister, but not from Gwyneth herself. Another

factor not taken into account was that someone – who, precisely, was never known – heard footsteps disappearing into the night during those fatal hours. Yet another theory is that Maye might have been sleepwalking and committed the murders while in that state, though that would not explain the blows he himself sustained.

Some years later, two local people who recalled the case well spoke to local historian Judy Chard. One was Leonard Pedrick, who brought the load of manure for which Maye had been waiting. According to him, Maye was known to have a quick temper and inclined to be unusually strict with his daughters. Nevertheless, there is some difference between a stern, unbending yet respectable patriarch and a psychopath hell-bent on eliminating his nearest and dearest. Even so, Pedrick had grave misgivings, remarking that he 'always felt there was an unhealthy atmosphere between himself and his daughters'. The other person was a lady who, like the Maye family, attended church regularly. She had sat in a pew with them on the Sunday before the killings and said that, despite the doctor's testimony, everyone was convinced that Maye was guilty as charged. Her own father knew him well and was never quite the same again after the case. Following the events of that night he had a nervous breakdown, and she was sure that it had been precipitated by the triple murder.

The 300 acres of land belonging to the farm were let to a Suffolk farmer, and in March 1937 the implements, equipment and some of the stock were sold. It was a sad end to a sorry and tragic case which left too many questions unanswered.

The police did not emerge from the business unscathed either. Young policemen joining the force in Devon for some years afterwards were lectured on the Maye case as a salutary lesson in how not to conduct a murder inquiry. Mugridge's errors of judgement and ill-considered words on arriving at the house had been counter-productive, and the judge admonished him in court for his having taken 'a view which might have been entirely wrong'.

According to one account, Maye left England and emigrated to Australia, where he died soon afterwards, though another says that he spent the rest of his life with his daughter Mary and her husband. The latter is more probable. He survived the terrible night of June 1936 by more than twenty years and died on 10 February 1957, aged ninety-one. As an inscription on the gravestone in St Mary's churchyard testifies, at last he could be reunited with his wife and daughters.

# 33
# HOLIDAY OF DEATH

Afomfter leaving school, Ernest John Moss joined the police force and was stationed at Brixham, where he settled down with his wife and their two children. When his marriage broke down, he left the house, resigned from his job and moved to Ilfracombe, where he found himself a house at Highfield Terrace. He worked first as an assistant at a company provision stores and then as a taxi driver.

While in Exeter on business one day he ran into Constance May ('Kitty') Bennett, an Exeter girl of eighteen whom he had already briefly met. She was living with her parents at Myrtle Road, Exeter. After leaving school she had obtained at post as a clerk in a local engineering firm, then worked at the Port House Laundry in Alphington Street. By the time Moss met Kitty he had moved again, to the seaside town of Woolacombe. Brooklyn, his new home, was an attractive bungalow with a veranda bowered in roses, close to the seashore.

He and Kitty became close friends, and at the end of July 1937 she went to stay with him, intending to be there for about three weeks. She wrote to her parents in Exeter to say how much she was enjoying herself, and would shortly be sending them some presents, including tobacco for her father. According to her mother, Kitty 'was our principal mainstay for the home'. She had left her job at the laundry, where she had been a valued employee, and her employers said they were sorry to lose her. It was the first holiday Kitty had ever had, Mrs Bennett told a journalist, and she said she thought it would do her good. 'We never had any trouble with her. A proper stay-at-home girl she was. But when the question of her going away on this occasion was discussed, she remarked, "Others have struck out in the world. Why shouldn't I?"'

From friends they doubtless became lovers, and marriage, after Moss's divorce came through, was part of the plan. For him, it was to be a new start after several unsatisfactory years. For her, the pure white maiden who had played the role of dutiful daughter and had probably never been allowed to be herself until now, it was a release from the shackles of a life at home, which she evidently longed to escape.

Alas for their hopes for a bright new future together, the ending was not to be a happy one. Perhaps Moss thought he had made a mistake in leaving his

*Kitty Bennett, as pictured in the* Western Morning News.

old life behind, suspected that Kitty was not the right woman for him, and still hoped for a reconciliation with his wife and children. At any rate, he was extremely depressed, and apparently decided the only way out was to take his own life, but he lacked the nerve or the conviction to do so. Then, on Saturday 7 August 1937, he picked up a double-barrelled gun and battered Kitty to death.

Almost at once he walked out of the house, went to the nearest police station and gave himself up. Officers accompanied him back to Brooklyn, where they found Kitty's fully dressed body on the bed. That evening her parents were taken by the police to Barnstaple to identify some of her belongings. An inquest was opened at Ilfracombe on 9 August and adjourned. The North Devon Coroner, Dr Ellis Pearson, confirmed that the cause of death was fracture of the skull. On the same day Moss was brought to Barnstaple police headquarters before the county justices, formally charged with murder, and remanded in custody.

He was tried at Exeter Assizes on 15 November. Mr G.D. Roberts and Mr J.D. Casswell appeared for the prosecution, Mr J.G. Trapnell and Mr H. Elam for the defence. Moss pleaded guilty to the murder charge, but the presiding judge, Mr Justice Hawke, tried to persuade him to take advantage of mitigating circumstances. He pointed out that counsel had been assigned to defend him, and asked if he thought he knew what he was doing when he attacked Kitty. The prisoner replied that he did. Referring to the defence counsel, Hawke said, 'I am given to understand that you desire that they should no longer represent you.' 'That is right, sir.' 'You understand that you are pleading guilty to having taken the life of this girl on purpose, by some deadly act of your own, done voluntarily and deliberately. You understand all that?' 'Yes, my lord.'

When Moss persisted in saying that he understood his plea would preclude any inquiry into questions as to the state of his mind, Hawke asked Roberts, 'What can I do about this?' Roberts said he thought there were two courses open to him. One was to accept the plea. The other, acting on precedent, was to order a plea of 'not guilty' to be entered and the case to be tried. The judge said that if he thought the prisoner did not understand what he was doing, he could enter a plea for him. 'But is there authority', he asked, 'for the proposition that I can enter a plea for him if I am satisfied that he knows what he is doing? Do you think it is in my powers to enter a plea of not guilty for him? I have grave doubts about it.'

Roberts said he did not think it could be said that his lordship did not have that power, and that nobody was allowed to advance a defence except the prisoner himself, provided it was clear that he was fit to plead and knew what he was doing. The judge asked Moss, 'You understand the consequence of your plea, do you not?' Again Moss answered that he did. It was as if he simply did not wish to live any longer and regarded his inevitable sentence as a release.

'Perhaps I may tell you,' the judge continued, 'you should know that I have seen certain mental reports about you. I do not say anything more about their effect than that there may be some doubt about your mental condition at the time, not at the moment. Do you think you had better plead not guilty, and

*Woolacombe, overlooking Barricane Shell Beach. Brooklyn, where Kitty Bennett was killed in August 1937, is among the bungalows overlooking the scene.*

let this trial proceed on such inquiries as arise? I make that appeal to you to do so, because there may be aspects of this matter which will not arise if you persist in your plea. Will you say not guilty and let this be thoroughly inquired into?'

Moss was adamant: he still intended to plead guilty. Rarely can any convicted murderer have come so close to what was, in effect, begging for execution. Turning to Roberts, the judge said that the Home Secretary had 'the most complete powers as to inquiry into this man's state of mind, whatever happens here. . . . I am afraid I see no alternative but to accept this plea. I am satisfied he knows what he is doing.' Roberts agreed, 'having regard to the attitude adopted and persisted in by the prisoner'. The judge then gave Moss a final chance to reconsider. 'Counsel has been assigned to defend you. I see them here. Do you think it would be better to have this matter inquired into? Do you still wish to plead guilty?'

Moss had no intention of changing his mind, and there was only one way the business could be concluded. The clerk of assize accordingly informed Moss that he stood convicted on his own confession of wilful murder. 'Have you anything to say why the Court should not pass upon you judgment of death, according to law?' 'No, sir', was the reply.

The judge donned the black cap, addressing him, 'I am satisfied you realise all the results of what you have done. It may be, I do not know, that you think by taking the course you are taking you are giving some sort of expiation; that you may have in your mind some idea that what you have done will enable you to have mercy hereafter. I don't know.' After a pause he added, 'If it be the fact that your mind has been injuriously affected by some disease of it, there will be those hereafter who will most carefully consider it. I shall make it my business, my duty, to make a special appeal to the Home Secretary to see that this is done, but no appeal from me is necessary. The law in this country is merciful, and the Home Secretary, one knows, takes the utmost care to consider all these cases. As you are determined, and as I am satisfied you know what you are doing, I have no alternative but to pass sentence upon you.'

'Thank you, my Lord,' said Moss, before turning in the dock and walking briskly down the steps, followed by two warders. It was as if he felt a sense of relief at knowing the agony of his earthly life would soon be over. He was hanged by Tom Pierrepoint and Stanley Cross at Exeter on 7 December, the last convicted murderer in Devon to be executed at the city gaol.

# 34

# MOTHER AND SON

## Torquay, 1938

These days, it is not uncommon to read of mercy killings, when an incurably ill person is put out of his or her misery by a close relative. It is therefore perhaps a matter of debate as to whether the violent death of Alice Smith at the hands of her son should really be viewed as murder.

In the summer of 1938 Alice Maud Smith and her son Norman lived in a three-bedroomed house in Hill Park Road, Torquay. They had been in residence for the last six years, with a cat and a canary for company. To most of their neighbours, Alice was just an ordinary, or perhaps a slightly eccentric, housewife. Others knew her for a time as a palmist, practising under the name of Madame Lorraine. In the eyes of Norman, her only child, she was an unhappy, downtrodden wife who needed protecting from her quarrelsome

*Hill Park Road, Torquay.* (© James Cosgrave)

husband, who was a labourer also called Norman. As a small boy, Norman junior became used to taking Alice's side and trying to defend her. In or about 1924, when Norman was fifteen, his father left home. The unhappy child grew to be an unhappy young man; Alice was not always the most grateful of mothers, and he suffered from her violent verbal lashings.

By the time Norman was an adult, Alice was in poor health. She drank heavily, was struck by abdominal pain and was suffering from cirrhosis of the liver. Her attitude to her son was alternately one of contempt or of intense affection. He obtained a clerical post with a firm of solicitors, and over a period of four or five years he managed to misappropriate a substantial sum of money from the firm. However, in his spare time he was a pillar of the local community, acting as scoutmaster for the 1st Torquay (St Marychurch) Boy Scouts, who were reputed to be one of the most active and successful groups in the district, and undertaking some voluntary work for the local church.

Though Norman was well respected in the area, it was inevitable that his financial activities at the office would be detected before long, and on Friday 26 August 1937 he was dismissed. That afternoon he found two people to witness the will he had just drawn up, which included the clause: 'I desire my body to be cremated with that of my darling mother and the ashes to be thrown into the sea off Petitor Beach.' Maybe he knew what was coming to him, and he must have had a presentiment that an increasingly insupportable situation at home was about to be resolved.

At this stage his mother, now aged fifty-four, was in increasing pain. Unable to sleep, she had more or less lost the will to carry on. On the afternoon after Norman's dismissal they went out for a walk, and in the early evening they took a drive together, during which she told him she could not endure any more

*Torquay Boy Scouts line up for inspection, 1960.* (Courtesy of Ted Gosling)

sleepless nights and she would rather kill herself. Back at home in the evening he got her two cups of hot milk for the night and followed her upstairs. She went into the bathroom and found herself a razor, but he was watching her and took it from her before she could do herself any harm. He then went downstairs again to prepare some food. As he was taking a frying pan and a rolling pin off the hook, he heard a bump and a shriek from upstairs. With the rolling pin still in his hand he ran up to see what was wrong, and saw her kneeling at the foot of the bed with blood running down her face.

Looking at him, she shouted, 'For God's sake, Norman, finish me quick.' Without hesitation, he hit her two or three blows with the rolling pin. She did not make a sound and he did not know how much effect his actions had had, so he pressed his thumb on her throat and held it there. After he was sure she was dead, he cleared up the mess in the bedroom and placed the stained clothes on the fire downstairs, along with some correspondence belonging to him and to his mother.

Next morning he drove to the Torbay hospital and picked up two nurses, both sisters. They went for a drive with him, and he told them that his mother was still in bed. Early in the afternoon he went to Torquay police station and told Sergeant Taylor that he had killed his mother. 'Don't look alarmed,' he said, explaining how he had done it and that she had been in ill-health for some years.

The sergeant accompanied him back to the house where he found Alice lying in bed with a bloodstained towel under her head. Norman said rather poignantly that after she was dead he had dressed her in a clean pair of pyjamas, washed her face, combed her hair and put her to bed. He then took the sergeant to the scullery and showed him the rolling pin: 'It's just as I used it, it's not been washed since.' Later he added that he had hit her twice and put the towel on the pillow to stop the blood. He was then taken back to the police station where he showed the officers the will he had made on the Friday. Detective Sergeant Roper was there, and Norman admitted he had no regrets about what he had done – 'She's better off now than she has been for the past twelve years.' When Alice's body was examined by doctors, one of their number, Dr Maurice Lees, confirmed that death was due to three injuries to the head and a fractured skull.

Roper charged and cautioned Smith, who made a full statement about the events leading up to Alice's death, as well as the fatal deed and his putting her to bed afterwards. He ended by saying again that he had no regrets about what he had done because his mother had suffered such terrible agonies for the past two or three years. 'She is at rest now, and I know she will not blame me for what I have done.' The cat went to the RSPCA home at Torre and Sergeant Taylor took the canary.

The news of Mrs Smith's death devastated the local community. The family's vicar, the Revd J. Johnston, was probably more shocked than anyone else. He told reporters that Norman had 'always been a very straight-living fellow, and I understand he has been a wonderful son to his invalid mother.'

Under his full name, Norman John Walker William Smith, the defendant, described as a law clerk, appeared before the police court on 23 September and was committed for trial. Opening the case for the prosecution, Mr G.R. Paling read passages from the statement the prisoner had made to the police. He said that Smith claimed he had tried to prevent his mother from taking her life, and then drew attention to the will, which stated that he wanted his body to be cremated with that of his mother. The prisoner, he went on, had decided that his mother's body would be available for such a process at the same time as his. As the document was dated 26 August, the day he was dismissed from his job with the solicitors and the day before the killing, he suggested that Smith had decided on the Friday evening that he intended to commit the offence 'and possibly some other', namely suicide.

The prisoner's father, Norman Smith, who lived nearby in St Edmunds Road, took the witness stand to say that he had not lived with his wife for the last twelve years, and that he had made no financial provision for her. He affirmed that Norman junior was the only child; 'he was a good boy, and always had been'. Beyond leaving those present to draw the obvious conclusion that his son had supported his ailing mother for want of any financial assistance from a self-centred bolter of a husband, Norman snr added nothing materially to the proceedings.

Brief statements were also made by Stella Harvey, one of the nurses whom Norman jnr had taken for a ride on the Sunday morning; by Thomas Boon and George Wilson, who had signed the will; by Alice's regular doctor, Dr William Forrest; and by Detective Sergeant Roper. The bench granted the defence the service of leading counsel at the trial, in addition to that of junior counsel.

When the case went before Exeter Assizes on 8 November, the prisoner was not called to give evidence. There was only one witness for the defence, a nerve and mental illness specialist. The counsel for the prosecution were Mr J.D. Casswell and Mr J.T. Malony, and for the defence Mr W. Blake Odgers and Mr H. Elam. After reading to the court Smith's statement, which he had made to the police, Mr Casswell asked whether the defendant's testimony regarding putting an end to his mother's agonies was consistent with his action in drafting his will with a clause relating to the joint cremation of his mother and himself. The prosecution submitted they were entirely inconsistent, and that the prisoner had made up his mind that both were to die – but he lacked the courage to complete the deed by killing himself.

Mr Blake Odgers told the jury that, owing to the perfectly frank and straightforward statements made by the accused, the facts were hardly in dispute at all. The defence of the charge, he declared, was that whatever state Mr Smith's mind might be in at present, at the time he carried out the killing he was not sane. As counsel for the defence, he would have to satisfy them by evidence that at the time Norman Smith was suffering from a disease of the mind which meant either that he was unable to know the difference between right and wrong, or that he did not realise what he did was wrong.

Dr R.N. Craig, mental illness and nerve specialist, said that Smith had had a very unhappy childhood. His upbringing was one of the most potent causes of mental instability later in life. Despite medical attention, Mrs Smith's health had become progressively worse, and her excessive consumption of alcohol brought about a growing mental change. Her son had been subjected to an ever-increasing degree of mental tension and uncertainty, from which he was able to obtain no relief. Finally, with no employment and no money, he had reached a complete impasse from which there was no escape, except for him to kill his mother and then take his own life.

When the judge asked whether Dr Craig meant that Smith's attitude was that his mother should have been killed and his own life ended, the latter replied that he thought the accused still had a strong suicidal urge. He said he would like to refer to an incident which had happened while the accused was in prison. Smith was distressed because he had asked to receive Communion and the chaplain, not surprisingly, found it difficult to agree until Smith had repented of his actions. He replied that he could not repent of something which to him was not wrong. When questioned by Mr Elam, Dr Craig said that Smith's reaction showed a disease of the mind, affecting his reasoning powers. Smith, he emphasised, was totally under the influence of his mother, and this accounted for the absence of agitation or emotion. He was carrying out something which she wished him to do. 'It was a pleasure and not a distasteful and unpleasant business.' From the moment he left the kitchen, Dr Craig continued, he was surely no longer responsible for his actions, and the decision to end his mother's life had been arrived at the previous day.

Three other medical officers stated that they had found no evidence that Smith was mentally abnormal. One, Dr Preece, medical officer of Exeter prison, said that the accused was of above average intelligence, and he could not agree that there had been any evidence of delusion or hallucinations.

The judge presumably felt otherwise. In summing up, he told the jury that it was 'a peculiarly sad case. It may be that it will not make very much difference to the accused what verdict you come to.' If they returned a verdict of guilty but insane, they must be satisfied not only that the accused was suffering from defect of reason, but that the defect of reason arose from disease of the mind. 'Does it not show that he was simply putting his mother out of her misery? Does it not show that he thought it right to kill her out of compassion because he thought she was suffering so much? Is that insanity? Is it defective reason coming from disorder of the mind to hold that view and carry it out? That is the question for you to consider.'

The jury retired for an hour and three-quarters. Compassion won the day, and they concluded that in effect Smith had killed his mother out of mercy. They returned a verdict of guilty but insane. Smith was ordered to be detained at His Majesty's pleasure.

# 35

# THE FATAL KISS

## Plymouth, 1952

The Second World War placed a strain on many marriages, one typical casualty being that of Thomas Eames and his first wife. They tied the knot when he was in his late teens, shortly before the outbreak of hostilities in 1939. The following year he joined the army and his wife left him, though the marriage was never dissolved. After demobilisation he found himself work as a labourer. In 1947 he met Muriel Elsie Bent and went through a bigamous marriage with her. At the time he was aged twenty-six and she was five years younger. After being convicted of bigamy, he served two days in prison. On his release the couple lived with his parents until they found a house of their own at 3 Northumberland Terrace, West Hoe, in Plymouth, and had a child.

The relationship soon broke down – they quarrelled throughout most of the time they lived together – and at length Muriel decided she had had enough. When she found herself a boyfriend, she moved out of their home. Thomas saw her and her new man together in Plymouth on at least a couple of occasions; jealous by nature, he could not put up with the situation indefinitely. On 23 February 1952 he called on his brother-in-law, Ronald William Greep, at Greenbank Avenue, and said there had been 'an upset' between them. Greep thought he seemed in a very nervous state, under great strain. He was unable to eat or sleep properly, and was suffering from severe stomach trouble. Three days later Eames asked Muriel to call round at the old house to collect a letter, and she readily agreed.

On the following day, 27 February, he took a 5½-inch table knife round to his place of work, borrowed a file from one of his workmates, and spent about half an hour sharpening what had been a single-bladed kitchen implement into a two-edged dagger. He then returned home and waited for her to call round. When she arrived, he asked Muriel if she was planning to marry her boyfriend. She said she was, and he told her she would not. According to a statement he later gave, 'I said: "If I cannot have you, nobody else will." She kissed me. As she was kissing me it flashed in my head, "Now is the time." I drew the knife out of my pocket and stabbed her in the back while kissing her. She said "Goodbye." I thought she was not quite dead so I stabbed her again so that she would not linger.'

*Northumberland Terrace, near Plymouth Hoe.* (© Kim Van der Kiste)

Muriel's death was instantaneous. (Dr M.R. Thomas of Greenbank Hospital later recorded that there were two wounds on the deceased's body, and that death would have taken place within a few seconds.) Next Eames contacted his brother-in-law, Ronald William Greep, confessed to what he had done, and asked Greep to accompany him to the Octagon police station so that he could give himself up. After being cautioned, Eames admitted to Inspector Harold Poole that he had killed his wife by stabbing her. 'The knife is on top of the cupboard. It was jealousy made me do it. She left me for another man. I sharpened the knife this morning.' As he was unable to read or write, apart from signing his name, he dictated a full statement to Detective Superintendent W.A. McConnach.

Charged with murder, he appeared at Exeter Assizes on 23 June before Mr Justice Lynskey and pleaded not guilty. For the defence, Mr N.F. Fox Andrews and Mrs H.S. Ruttle tried to show that he was insane at the time of the murder, owing to the effects of worry, stress and an inability to eat properly. Ronald Greep confirmed that he had seen his brother-in-law on several evenings, and had noticed a deterioration in him. He seemed to be increasingly worked up with each passing day, and had told Ronald of his insomnia and severe stomach pains. On the evening that Muriel was killed, he briefly seemed his old self again, said his stomach pain was gone, and then told Greep what he had done. Eames's brother, Cyril, who lived nearby at Clarence Street, said his brother had always been 'a kindly, decent fellow, affectionate by nature'.

Superintendent McConnach produced the statement that had been dictated by the prisoner, and said he had problems with expressing himself. When asked by the judge if he thought the prisoner knew what he was saying and doing, McConnach replied in the affirmative. Fox Andrews mentioned that Eames's relatives called him 'a quiet and gentle fellow, would you from what you have seen of him agree?' The superintendent again answered 'Yes'. 'He is the reverse of the violent character?' 'Yes.'

Next Fox Andrews cross-examined the prisoner, who said that he loved Muriel Bent and their child, and that he could not clearly remember the night she died. 'You don't dispute now that you killed her in fact?' 'No.' 'At the time when you struck her did you know what you were doing?' 'I did not know before, but I did after, sir.'

For the prosecution, the Hon. Ewan Montagu and Mr J.F.E. Stephenson described the case as 'rather a simple one as regards the actual killing'. According to Montagu, it was 'a perfectly clear, intentional, deliberate killing out of jealousy'. Detective Sergeant L.J. Isaacs, when cross-examined by Fox Andrews, read from a letter which he said he understood Eames had dictated and had written for him on 26 February, addressed to Muriel Bent's father. It explained that Eames had asked her to marry him again (even though in the eyes of the law he was still married to the first Mrs Eames), but she had said she did not want to be his wife any longer. He begged her father to come to Plymouth so he could explain the situation and prove to him that he had never ill-treated her, in spite of whatever she might have told him to the contrary. The letter concluded: 'If she does not take any notice of you I am afraid she will be lost to us both in the way she is carrying on.'

As in so many other murder cases, some of the evidence dwelt on the prisoner's state of mind at the time of the killing. Dr J.T. Dunkerley, a part-time medical officer at Exeter prison, said that while in his cell Eames had said that when he was a child, he saw a vision which he 'took to be Our Lord'. When he saw it he was suffering from sores on his foot, and when he went to bathe them the next morning after his visions, he found that they had completely healed. Nevertheless, this was hardly proof of insanity, and when he was cross-examined by Montagu, Dunkerley said that in his view Eames was sane. It was a view supported by Mr M.R.P. Williams, a medical officer at Bristol prison. He admitted that the prisoner had the average intelligence of a cross-section of the public over sixteen years of age, but he was more or less illiterate; this hardly amounted to insanity.

Mr Fox Andrews submitted that if the prisoner was unaware of the consequences of his actions when he drove the knife into the victim's back, it did not matter if he contemplated doing it or if the realisation came to him after the deed was done. 'The question is whether at the time he struck the blow he knew what he was doing,' he concluded. 'If, looking at the whole of the evidence, you take the view that at that moment he did not know what he was doing, then you will be entitled to and it would be your duty to return a verdict of guilty but insane.'

In his summing up the judge pointed out that Eames could have been temporarily insane at the time of the killing. Two doctors had given evidence that he was sane, but it was possible for people who were worried and sleepless and had not eaten properly to commit acts of violence without knowing it. The jury thought otherwise, and believed that Eames had planned to murder Muriel. As he had gone to such effort to prepare the weapon, such a claim was difficult to contest, and they found him guilty, but added a recommendation for mercy. The case was referred to the Home Secretary, who maintained that there were 'insufficient grounds for recommending any interference with the due course of law'. When he went to the scaffold at Bristol gaol on 15 July, to be hanged by Albert Pierrepoint and Robert Stewart, Eames had to be dragged fighting and kicking. He struggled all the way to the drop.

Shortly after a new Labour government came to power in October 1964 Sydney Silverman, Labour Member of Parliament for Nelson & Colne and a lifelong campaigner for an end to capital punishment in Britain, was assured by the Home Secretary that there would never be another execution by hanging under a Labour administration. His Murder (Abolition of the Death Penalty) Bill passed its first reading in December, and royal assent was given to the act in November 1965, suspending capital punishment for murder for five years. In December 1969 a further parliamentary vote reaffirmed the decision that it should be permanently abolished. To Thomas Eames belonged the dubious distinction of being the last Devon murderer to be executed.

# BIBLIOGRAPHY AND REFERENCES

Where individual newspapers or journal articles have been consulted for specific cases, these are cited in the list below. Most of the books that follow have been consulted in the research for several chapters, and I feel it more suitable to list them thus. Certain websites have also been used, though as these have a habit of disappearing from the internet without warning, to avoid frustration to the reader who wants to know more, I have not cited them.

NEWSPAPER AND JOURNAL REFERENCES

2. Set up to Pay the Price, 1811
*The Times*, 12 August 1811

3. The Violent Sailor, 1816
*Western Flying Post*, 14 November 1816, 25 March 1817

4. The Fatal Triangle, 1818
*Exeter Flying Post*, 26 March 1818; *The Times*, 26 March 1818

5. The Killing of a Mother-to-Be, 1823
*Exeter Flying Post*, 17 and 31 July 1823

6. Friend by Name but Not by Nature, 1827
*The Times*, 24, 27 and 31 March 1827

7. 'By the Lord's Mercy You'll Hang Me Innocent!', 1829
*The Times*, 17 and 20 August 1829

8. The Murderer and the Book of Poetry, 1830
*Exeter Flying Post*, 29 October 1829, 31 March 1830

9. An Infanticide, 1832
*The Times*, 29 March 1832

10. Death after the Fair, 1835
*The Times*, 1 August 1836

11. A Gamekeeper's Violent End, 1839
*The Times*, 2 February, 25 March 1839

12. Death of a Tax Collector, 1853
*The Times*, 9 February 1853; *Somerset County Gazette*, 30 December 1961

13. The Glove-maker and the Chimney-sweep, 1854
*The Times*, 26 and 29 July, 5 August 1854

14. The Torquay Baby Farmer, 1865
*The Times*, 20 March, 29 July, 10 and 12 August, 25 November 1865, 15 March 1866

15. The Shoemaker, His Wife and Her Lover, 1865
*The Times*, 19 and 29 March 1866; *Tavistock Gazette*, 29 March 1866; *Western Daily Mercury*, 17 March 1866; *Western Morning News*, 7 November 1865, 17 March 1866

16. Extra Drill Led Him to Kill, 1869
*Western Morning News*, 2 August, 23 September 1869; *The Times*, 23 September 1869

18. The Man They Could Not Hang, 1884
*The Times*, 5 February 1885; *Western Morning News*, 5 February 1885

19. The Riverkeeper and the Poachers, 1887
*The Times*, 1 August 1887, 31 May 1922; *Western Morning News*, 1, 2 and 9 August 1887

20. Atrocity at Peter Tavy, 1892
*The Times*, 15 and 30 November, 1 December 1892, 11 and 29 March 1893; *Western Morning News*, 15, 17, 18 and 30 November, 1 December 1892, 10, 29 and 30 March 1893

21. The Paranoid Painter, 1900
*Western Morning News*, 7 July, 16 November 1900; *The Times*, 17 November 1900

24. An Unsuitable Youth, 1908
*The Times*, 19 November 1908, 12 March 1909; *Western Morning News*, 18–20 November 1908, 12 March 1909; *Western Evening Herald*, 18 November 1908, 11 March 1909

25. The Work-shy Ex-Sailor, 1912
*Western Morning News*, 11, 27 and 29 November 1912, 4 February 1913

26. The Thwarted Naval Stoker, 1913
*Western Morning News*, 20 and 29 October 1913, 4 February 1914

27. The Soldier and the Schoolgirl, 1916
*Western Morning News*, 21 June, 4 and 13 November 1916; *The Times*, 28 November 1916

28. The Killing of Sister Catherine, 1916
*The Times*, 8 August, 4 November 1916; *Western Morning News*, 8 August, 4 November 1916

29. The Fatal Attraction of Two Cousins, 1920
*Western Evening Herald*, 23 September, 9 and 10 November 1920; *Western Morning News*, 24 September, 10 November 1920

30. Shooting on the Moor, 1927
*The Times*, 7 July and 19 November 1927; *Western Morning News*, 22 and 23 July, 2 November 1927

31. The Body in the Allotment, 1927
*Western Morning News*, 28 and 29 June, 3 and 19 November 1927; *The Times*, 7 July, 19 November 1927

32. Massacre at West Charleton, 1936
*The Times*, 30 and 31 July, 10 November 1936; *Western Morning News*, 13, 15 and 16 June, 30 and 31 July, 10 November 1936; Judy Chard, 'Triple slaying at Croft Farm, West Charleton', *Devon Life*, October 1998

33. Holiday of Death, 1937
*The Times*, November 1937; *Western Morning News*, 9 and 10 August, 16 November 1937

34. Mother and Son, 1938
*The Times*, 30 August, 24 September, 9 November 1938; *Western Morning News*, 29 and 30 August, 24 September, 9 November 1938

35. The Fatal Kiss, 1952
*The Times*, 16 July 1952; *Western Morning News*, 24 June, 16 July 1952

## BOOKS

Anon, *St Petrock's Church, South Brent*, Plymouth, A.C. Brown, 1951

Chard, Judy, *Tales of the Unexplained in Devon*, Exeter, Obelisk, 1986

——, *Murder and Mystery in Devon*, Chudleigh, Orchard, 1994

——, *Devon Tales of Mystery and Murder*, Newbury, Countryside, 2001

Clayhidon Local History Group, *Clayhidon: A Parish on the Blackdowns*, Clayhidon Local History Group, 2000

Dell, Simon, *The Beat on Western Dartmoor: A celebration of 150 years of the policing of Tavistock*, Newton Abbot, Forest, 1997

Eddleston, John J., *The Encyclopedia of Executions*, London, John Blake, 2004

Engel, Howard, *Lord High Executioner: An unashamed look at hangmen, headsmen, and their kind*, London, Robson, 1998

Evans, Stewart P., *Executioner: The chronicles of a Victorian hangman*, Stroud, Sutton, 2004

Fielding, Steve, *The Hangman's Record, Vol. 1, 1868–1899; Vol. 2, 1900–1929; Vol. 3, 1930–1964*, Beckenham, CBD, 1994–2005

Harrison, John Grant, *The Penalty Was Death: Nineteenth-century crime and executions in Devon*, Tiverton, Halsgrove, 1997

Harrison, Paul, *Devon Murders*, Newbury, Countryside, 1992

Holgate, Mike, and Waugh, Ian, *The Man They Could Not Hang: The true story of John Lee*, Stroud, Sutton, 2005

James, Ann, *Murders and Mysteries in Devon*, Exeter, Obelisk, 1996

Trist, Edward, *Take Cover: The wartime memories of a Devon policeman, 1938–1946*, Newton Abbot, Forest, 2001

Wall, Greg, *The Book of South Brent*, Tiverton, Halsgrove, 2005

Wilson, Colin, introduced by, *Murder in the Westcountry*, Bodmin, Bossiney, 1975

# INDEX